Vega

106 Tasty & Nourishing Recipes For A Ketogenic Vegan Diet

By Karen McAdams & Marian Lee

Table of Contents

INTRODUCTION 2

BREAKFAST RECIPES 3

  1. FRUITY CHIA PUDDING 3

  2. GREEN AVOCADO PANCAKES 5

  3. SAVORY CREPES WITH MUSHROOM & ASPARAGUS FILLING 7

  4. LIMEY WAFFLES WITH COCONUT CREAM 10

  5. EGGPLANT GUAC STACK 12

  6. MUSHROOMS IN SPINACH-COCONUT CREAM 14

  7. RICH CAROB PROTEIN SMOOTHIE 16

  8. COCONUT CAULIFLOWER PORRIDGE 17

  9. BREAD WITH HERBED BUTTER 19

  10. ALMOND BUTTER & RED CURRANT MUFFINS 21

  11. TOASTED COCONUT FLAKES WITH ALMOND MILK 23

  12. BREAKFAST SMOOTHIE BOWL 25

  13. HIGH-PROTEIN HEMP SEED PORRIDGE 26

  14. LOW-CARB CHIA AND HEMP SEEDS PORRIDGE 28

  15. QUINOA BREAKFAST BOWL 30

LUNCH RECIPES **32**

  16. PALM HEART TACOS 32

  17. NOODLES WITH PESTO 34

  18. "SAUSAGES" WITH AIOLI 36

  19. CAULIFLOWER SALAD 38

  SERVE WARM.21. STUFFED PORTABELLA WITH NUT PATE 41

  22. SAVORY CREPES WITH MUSHROOM CREAM 44

  23. CRUST-LESS QUICHE 46

  24. VEGGIE FRITTERS WITH AVOCADO 48

  25. CREAMY CAULIFLOWER SOUP 50

  26. CURRY CAULIFLOWER RICE 52

  27. ZUCCHINI NOODLES WITH VEGAN CHEESE SAUCE 54

  28. ASIAN-STYLE GREEN BEANS WITH WALNUT BUTTER 55

  29. COLOURFUL WALNUT TACOS 57

  30. SAUTÉED BRUSSEL SPROUTS WITH RADICCHIO AND ALMONDS 59

  31. ALMOND & COCONUT ASPARAGUS 61

  32. SAUTÉED QUICK LUNCH VEGGIES 63

  33. CUCUMBER SALAD 65

  34. CAULIFLOWER SUMMER SALAD 67

  35. FENNEL AND GREEN BEANS PESTO SALAD 69

  36. BABY SPINACH, MUSHROOMS AND NUTS SALAD 71

37. Roasted Vegetables, Tofu & Pumpkin Seeds Salad 73

38. Kale, Avocado & Grilled Tempeh Salad...76

DINNER RECIPES **78**

39. Keto Vegan Falafel 78

40. Italian Baked Mushrooms.. 80

41. Avocado & Spinach Gazpacho 82

42. Healthy Green Tabbouleh 84

43. Olive Cauliflower Non-Meatballs... 86

44. Veggie Pizza Deluxe 88

45. Creamy "Cauli Rice" With Spinach.. 90

46. Eggplant & Zucchini Stack 91

47. Eggplant Fingers With Macadamia Hummus 93

48. Tofu Salad 95

49. Cauliflower and Cashew Nuts Indian Style..97

50. Grilled Avocado Stuffed with Broccoli and Tofu 99

51. Eggplant and Coconut Milk Curry with Cauliflower "Rice" 101

52. Pan-Seared Tempeh Steak with Roasted Cabbage and Walnuts 103

53. Scrambled Tofu with Guacamole 106

54. Cauliflower Couscous with Roasted Vegetables..109

55. Tempeh Curry Laksa Style with Kelp Noodles 111

56. Walnut Stuffed Eggplant with Rocket Salad 114

57. Broccoli and Zucchini Patties with Avocado and Walnut Salad 117

58. Broccoli Bisque with a Twist...120

59. Cream of Spinach Soup 122

60. Green Cauliflower Soup 124

61. Winter Italian Minestrone 126

62. Indian-Style Green Pepper, Courgettes, and Spinach Soup.............................128

EXTRAS **130**

63. Cucumber Bites 130

64. Broccoli Crispy Bread...132

65. Roasted Pumpkin Seeds 134

66. Multi Seeds Crackers 136

68. Tahini Dressing...139

69. Lemon & Mustard Vinaigrette..140

70. Cheesy Sauce.. 141

71. Chimichurri Style Sauce 142

72. Peanut Sauce 144

73. Spicy Almond & Garlic Dip 145

74. Cauliflower Hummus 146

75. Eggplant & Walnut Spread...148

76. Coconut Yogurt Dip 150

77. Olive Tapenade 151

78. Chunky Rocket Spread 152

SNACKS **153**

79. Avocado Slices 153

80. Kale Chips With Dip 155

81. Almond Butter With Celery Sticks..157

82. Palm Fingers 158

83. Avocado Mushroom Bombs 160

84. Ketogenic Tofu Bites 161

85. Zucchini Rolls With Nut Butter 163

86. Fried Guacamole 165

87. Green Smoothie 167

88. Icy Pops 168

89. Avocado & Raspberry Smoothie 169

90. Strawberry Coconut Smoothie.. 170

91. Thai Style Coconut Shake 171

92. Frozen Berry Shake 172

DESSERTS...**173**

93. Almond Butter Balls...173

94. Cocoa Pumpkin Fudge...175

95. Coconut Vanilla Panna Cotta 176

96. Creamy Vanilla Custard...177

97. Nutty Brownies 178

98. Refreshing "Fat Bombs" 180

99. Chocolate Hemp Mousse 181

100. Peanut Butter Cookies 182

101. Comfort Cups 184

102. Sweet Fritters With Lime 185

103. Quick Almond Butter Mousse... 187

104. Almond & Cocoa Mini Muffins 189

105. Almond Butter Squares..191

106. Coconut Bites... 193

© **Copyright 2018 by Pine Peak Publishing - All rights reserved.**

All material in this book is provided for your information only, and may not be construed as medical advice or instruction. No action or inaction should be taken based solely on the contents of this information; instead, readers should consult appropriate health professionals on any matter relating to their health and well-being

In no way is it legal to reproduce, duplicate, or transmit any part of this document in either electronic means or in printed format. Recording of this publication is strictly prohibited and any storage of this document is not allowed unless with written permission from the publisher. All rights reserved.

The information provided herein is stated to be truthful and consistent, in that any liability, in terms of inattention or otherwise, by any usage or abuse of any policies, processes, or directions contained within is the solitary and utter responsibility of the recipient reader.

Under no circumstances will any legal responsibility or blame be held against the publisher for any reparation, damages, or monetary loss due to the information herein, either directly or indirectly.

This document is geared towards providing exact and reliable information in regards to the topic and issue covered. The publication is sold with the idea that the publisher is not required to render accounting, officially permitted, or otherwise, qualified services. If advice is necessary, legal or professional, a practiced individual in the profession should be ordered.

Respective authors own all copyrights not held by the publisher. The information herein is offered for informational purposes solely, and is universal as so. The presentation of the information is without contract or any type of guarantee assurance.

The trademarks that are used are without any consent, and the publication of the trademark is without permission or backing by the trademark owner. All trademarks and brands within this book are for clarifying purposes only and are the owned by the owners themselves, not affiliated with this document.

Introduction

Veganism is an ideology based on the premise that all living creatures, including animals, should be respected, and that the killing and consumption of animals breaches this premise.

On the other hand, a ketogenic diet is a way of eating that was initially developed to minimize epileptic attacks. Later, it was discovered that it also helps a lot of people with weight loss.

A ketogenic diet promotes the consumption of mainly fats, and some protein, while maintaining very low levels of carbohydrates.

With a bit of planning, a vegan or ketogenic diet may not be difficult to follow by themselves. However, a vegan AND ketogenic diet... is that actually possible?

Yes!

While you'll undoubtedly be more limited in your food choices than most other people, a ketogenic vegan diet can still contain plenty of tasty and nutritious meals, and the proof is in this recipe book.

All of the included recipes are neatly numbered and organized into 6 different categories: Breakfast, Lunch, Dinner, Extras, Snacks and Desserts.

We hope you enjoy exploring the healthy, fatty goodness of the vegan keto world.

Happy cooking, and bon appétit!

Breakfast Recipes

1. Fruity Chia Pudding

Fruity Chia pudding is the perfect breakfast when you need something fruity, healthy, and fast. Don't be put off by the word 'fruity', though, as the carbs are still kept low.

Preparation time: 20 minutes

Serves: 1

Ingredients:

- ¾ cup unsweetened almond milk
- ¼ cup filtered water
- 2 tablespoons whole white Chia seeds
- 1 tablespoon almond butter
- ¼ cup fresh raspberries

Directions:

1. Mix almond milk, water, chia seeds, and almond butter in a bowl. If you prefer a smoother texture, blend the ingredients in a food blender instead.

2. Place the chia blend aside for 15 minutes.

3. In the meantime, blend raspberries in a food blender until smooth.

4. Strain the raspberry puree through a fine sieve and discard the seeds.

5. Spread the raspberry puree over the chia seed blend and serve.

6. For a more enjoyable experience, you can chill it before serving.

2. Green Avocado Pancakes

These wonderful pancakes are made with ripe avocado, spinach, and almond flour. These green beauties are some of the healthiest pancakes you'll ever try.

Preparation time: 10 minutes

Cooking time: 10 minutes

Serves: 4

Ingredients:
- 1 avocado
- 1 cup packed fresh baby spinach
- ½ cup almond flour
- ¼ teaspoon aluminum-free baking powder
- 1 flax egg*
- ¼ cup unsweetened almond milk
- 1 pinch Himalayan salt
- Coconut oil, to fry
-

*Flax egg: combine 2 tablespoons ground flax seeds with ¼ cup filtered water.

Place aside for 10 minutes or until thickened.

Directions:
1. Cut the avocado in half and remove the stone, then peel the avocado and cut into thin slices.

2. Place the avocado slices, spinach, flax egg, and almond milk in a food blender.

3. Blend until smooth. Transfer the batter into a medium bowl.

4. Fold in almond flour, baking powder, and salt.

5. Brush a non-stick skillet with melted coconut oil.

6. Pour 2-3 tablespoons of the batter into heated skillet.

7. Cook the pancakes on medium heat for 2 minutes. Flip gently (because the pancakes are very soft) and cook further for 2 minutes. Repeat with the remaining batter.

8. Serve warm with desired topping, or vegetables.

3. Savory Crepes With Mushroom & Asparagus Filling

Rich mushroom-asparagus filling, wrapped in thin, low-carb crepes and with decadent cashew-lemon sauce. A yummy start to the day!

Preparation time: 30 minutes

Cooking time: 20 minutes

Serves: 4

Ingredients:

For the crepes:

- 3 flax eggs*
- 1 ¼ cup blanched almond flour
- 1 tablespoon sifted coconut flour
- 1 teaspoon aluminum-free baking powder
- 1 cup unsweetened almond milk
- 2 tablespoons olive oil
- 1 pinch Himalayan salt

For the filling:

- 12 asparagus spears, trimmed
- 2 cups sliced mushrooms
- 3 tablespoons olive oil
- 1 sprig thyme, leaves removed
- 1 good pinch Himalayan salt

For the sauce;

- ¾ cup cashew butter
- 2 tablespoons lime juice
- 2 tablespoons lemon juice
- Salt, to taste
- White pepper, to taste

*Flax egg: combine 2 tablespoons ground flax seeds with ¼ cup filtered water. Place aside for 10 minutes or until thickened – equals one egg

Directions:

1. Make the sauce; place all ingredients in a food processor. Process the ingredients until smooth. Chill in a fridge before use.

2. Make the crepes; combine all the crepes ingredients in a bowl, except the olive oil. If needed add some more liquid.

3. Place the batter in a fridge for 30 minutes.

4. Heat some of the olive oil in a large pan.

5. Pour ¼ cup of the batter into the skillet and swirl the pan to distribute the batter evenly.

6. Cook until bubbles appear on the surface. Flip carefully and cook for 1 minute.

7. Repeat with remaining batter and keep the pancakes warm.

8. Make the filling; Heat olive oil in a pan over medium-high heat.

9. Add the sliced mushrooms and thyme and cook for 5 minutes.

10. Add the asparagus and cook until crisp-tender, for 2-3 minutes. Season with salt.

11. To assemble; place a pancake on a plate. Fill with some prepared filling and fold the pancake sides over the filling.

12. Drizzle with sauce and serve.

4. Limey Waffles With Coconut Cream

A refreshing, easy-to-make and satisfying breakfast experience.

Preparation time: 15 minutes

Cooking time: 10 minutes

Serves: 4

Ingredients:

For the waffles:

- 2 flax eggs*
- 2 tablespoons almond butter
- 1 ½ cups almond flour
- 2 tablespoons sifted coconut flour
- ¼ cup unsweetened almond milk
- 2 tablespoons lime juice
- Coconut oil, to brush the iron
- Desired sweetener, a combination of Erythritol and stevia, to taste

For the coconut cream:

- 15oz. can coconut milk (chilled in a fridge overnight)
- 1 teaspoon lime zest

*Flax egg: combine 2 tablespoons ground flax seeds with ¼ cup filtered water. Place aside for 10 minutes or until thickened – equals one egg

Directions:

1. Make the coconut cream; chill the coconut milk in a fridge overnight. Remove carefully from the fridge without shaking.

2. Open the can and remove the coconut cream solids. Place the coconut cream solids in a chilled bowl.

3. Beat coconut cream with lime zest, and desired sweetener using an electric mixer until fluffy. Store in a fridge until ready to use.

4. Make the waffles; combine all ingredients in a bowl.

5. Heat the waffle iron. Brush the iron gently with coconut oil.

6. Pour some of the prepared batter onto the iron and cook for 3-4 minutes.

7. Serve the waffles with a dollop of coconut cream.

5. Eggplant Guac Stack

This nutritious and satiating meal is made with eggplant and homemade guacamole. If you do it right, you'll end up with some crunchy-creamy goodness.

Preparation time: 40 minutes

Cooking time: 10 minutes

Serves: 4

Ingredients:

- 1 lb. eggplant, trimmed and sliced into ½-inch thick rounds
- ½ cup ground almonds
- ¼ cup ground macadamia nuts
- 1 teaspoon dried basil
- ½ cup flax seeds
- 1 cup filtered water
- ½ teaspoon Himalayan salt
- ½ teaspoon freshly ground white pepper
- ¼ cup melted coconut oil

For the guacamole:

- 2 small avocados
- 3 tablespoons lime juice
- 2 tablespoons freshly chopped chives
- Sea salt and pepper, to taste

Directions:

1. Make the guacamole; cut avocados in half and remove the stone.

2. Peel and slice the avocados and place into a small bowl.

3. Drizzle with lemon juice and season to taste with salt and pepper.

4. Mash the avocado with a fork and sprinkle with chives. Cover and store in a refrigerator until ready to use.

5. Make the eggplants; sprinkle eggplant slices with salt and place in a colander for 20 minutes.

6. Squeeze to remove excess liquid.

7. In a bowl, combine flax seeds and water.

8. Place aside for 15 minutes until thickened and gelatinous.

9. Combine almond flour with white pepper in a shallow dish, and place macadamia nuts in a separate shallow dish.

10. Heat coconut oil in a pan over medium-high heat.

11. Dredge eggplant slices in almond flour, dip into flax mixture and coat with macadamia nuts.

12. Place the eggplant slices into heated oil and fry for 2 minutes per side. Place onto a plate.

13. To assemble; spread some guacamole over one eggplant slice and sandwich with the second eggplant slice. Repeat with remaining slices and guacamole.

14. Serve warm.

6. Mushrooms In Spinach-Coconut Cream

Mushrooms and spinach pair perfectly, and this dish is proof of it. With the addition of tofu, it's a bit higher in protein than most other meals.

Preparation time: 10 minutes

Cooking time: 15 minutes

Serves: 4

Ingredients:

- ½ (15oz.) package silken tofu
- 1 ½ lb. sliced brown mushrooms
- 3 tablespoons coconut oil
- Sea salt, to taste

For the spinach:

- ½ lb. baby spinach
- 2 minced garlic cloves
- ½ cup unsweetened coconut cream
- 2 tablespoons coconut oil
- 1 pinch nutmeg
- Sea salt and black pepper, to taste

Directions:

1. Prepare the mushrooms; heat coconut oil in a medium pan over medium-high heat.

2. Add mushrooms and season to taste.

3. Cook the mushrooms for 6-7 minutes, stirring until soft.

4. In the meantime, mash the silken tofu with a fork.

5. Top the mushrooms with silken tofu and cook for 3-4 minutes.

6. Place aside and keep warm.

7. Make the spinach; heat coconut oil in a medium pan over medium-high heat.

8. Add garlic and cook until fragrant, for 30-40 seconds.

9. Toss in spinach and cook until wilted.

10. Add the coconut cream, nutmeg, and season to taste.

11. Stir well and remove from heat. Place the mushrooms and tofu in a bowl. Top with spinach.

7. Rich Carob Protein Smoothie

Smoothie is a perfect "fast food" you can prepare within only a few minutes. With a careful combination of ingredients, smoothies will fill you up for a long time, just like any other breakfast.

Preparation time: 5 minutes

Serves: 1 big smoothie

Ingredients:

- ¼ cup almond or coconut milk
- ¼ cup water
- 2 tablespoon cocoa butter
- 2 tablespoons unsweetened coconut cream
- 1 tablespoon carob powder
- 1 scoop mixed plant protein powder or soy protein powder
- 1 tablespoon macadamia oil or MCT oil
- ½ cup ice
- 4 drops Stevia
- ½ teaspoon Ceylon cinnamon

Directions:

1. Place all ingredients in a food blender.

2. Blend until smooth.

3. Serve immediately.

8. Coconut Cauliflower Porridge

Sometimes, you just need some comfort food for breakfast, and what is more comforting than warm bowl of porridge?

Preparation time: 10 minutes + inactive time

Cooking time: 10 minutes

Serves: 4

Ingredients:

- ½ head cauliflower, just florets, discard stems
- ¼ cup chia seeds
- ¾ cup coconut flakes
- 3 tablespoons coconut oil
- 1 ½ cup coconut milk
- ½ teaspoon Ceylon cinnamon
- Sweetener, like stevia to taste

Directions:

1. Preheat oven to 425F and line a baking sheet with baking paper.

2. Place cauliflower florets in a food processor with 1 tablespoon coconut oil.

3. Process until the cauliflower is rice-like in consistency.

4. Spread the cauliflower onto lined baking sheet and roast for 8-10 minutes.

5. In the meantime, combine chia seeds, coconut flakes, 1 cup coconut milk, and cinnamon in a bowl.

6. Add the cauliflower and give it a good stir. Cover and refrigerate for at least two hours.

7. Just before serving, combine remaining coconut oil, remaining coconut milk, and desired amount of Stevia in a food blender.

8. Blend until emulsified.

9. Pour the emulsified coconut oil over the cauliflower and stir gently. Serve immediately.

9. Bread With Herbed Butter

A lot of people who go on ketogenic diets really miss the consistency of freshly-baked bread. If you're one of them, this recipe will help allcviate some of your cravings.

Give this a try with some fresh avocado to serve, and you won't be disappointed!

Preparation time: 20 minutes

Cooking time: 60 minutes

Serves: 10 slices

Ingredients:

For the buns:
- ½ cup drained firm tofu
- 3 tablespoons ground flax seeds
- ¾ cup coconut milk
- ½ cup psyllium husk
- 1 teaspoon aluminum-free baking powder
- 1 good pinch Himalayan salt

For the butter:
- 4 tablespoons blanched almond flour
- 1 teaspoon nutritional yeast
- ¼ cup unsweetened almond milk or soy milk
- ½ cup melted and cooled coconut oil
- 2 tablespoons extra-virgin olive oil
- ½ teaspoon cider vinegar
- ½ teaspoon Himalayan salt

- 1 teaspoon fresh chopped thyme
- 1 teaspoon fresh chopped basil

To serve:

- 1 pitted, peeled, and sliced avocado

Directions:

1. Make the butter; blend almonds, nutritional yeast, almond milk, vinegar, herbs, and salt in a food blender until smooth.

2. While the blender is running on low, add coconut oil, followed by extra-virgin olive oil.

3. Continue blending until you have a velvety mixture. Transfer into a freezer-friendly glass jar and apply the lid.

4. Freeze until you make buns.

5. Make the buns; Preheat oven to 350F and line a baking sheet with a parchment paper.

6. Place the drained tofu in a food blender. Blend until smooth.

7. Add the remaining ingredients and blend until combined.

8. Drop the batter into mounds on a baking sheet. Bake for 55-60 minutes or until browned.

9. Serve warm with herbed butter and slices of avocado.

10. Almond Butter & Red Currant Muffins

Sweet, fluffy, and made with delicious red currants. A gourmet-like breakfast experience.

Preparation time: 15 minutes

Cooking time: 22 minutes

Serves: 12 muffins

Ingredients:

- ¾ cup coconut flour
- ¾ cup almond flour
- ½ cup almond butter
- 1 teaspoon aluminum-free baking soda
- ½ cup fresh red currants
- ½ cup almond milk
- 2 tablespoons coconut oil
- 2 flax eggs*
- Stevia + Erythritol, to taste
- 1 teaspoon pure vanilla extract

*Flax egg: combine 2 tablespoons ground flax seeds with ¼ cup filtered water. Place aside for 10 minutes or until thickened.

Directions:

1. Preheat oven to 350F and line 12-hole muffin tin with paper liners.

2. In a medium bowl, whisk together coconut flour, almond flour, and baking soda.

3. Make the flax eggs and place aside.

4. In a separate bowl, whisk together almond butter, almond milk, coconut oil, Stevia, Erythritol, vanilla, and flax eggs.

5. Fold the dry ingredients into the wet ingredients and stir to combine. If you feel the batter is too dry, add some almond milk.

6. Gently fold in red currants and divide batter between muffin liners.

7. Bake the muffins for 20-22 minutes.

8. Serve at room temperature.

11. Toasted Coconut Flakes with Almond Milk

This is a delicious meal to start your day with. The toasted coconut flakes are a great substitute for regular cereals, which are usually loaded with sugar.

You can toast the coconut in a big batch, and keep it in an airtight container in the cupboard, ready to use at any time.

Preparation time: 15 minutes

Cooking time: 5 minutes

Serves: 5

Ingredients:

- 1 lb. flaked coconut
- 1 tbsp. ground cinnamon
- 1/2 cup unsweetened almond milk
- 1 tbsp. dried cranberries
- 2 medium-sized to large strawberries - sliced
- 1 sheet of baking paper
- 1 tsp. coconut oil

Preparation:

1. Preheat oven to 350F.

2. Line a baking tray with a sheet of baking paper. Grease the paper with coconut oil.

3. Pour the coconut flakes over the baking paper.

4. When the oven reaches the temperature, put the flakes in the oven and bake for five minutes. Keep an eye on the flakes the whole time as you do not want them to burn.

5. Shuffle the flakes around and keep baking until they are a little golden and lightly toasted.

6. Take the flakes out of the oven and sprinkle with cinnamon. Taste and if you like you can add more cinnamon.

7. Put 1 cup of the coconut flakes into a bowl. Sprinkle with the cranberries and add the unsweetened Almond milk.

8. Add the strawberries for extra freshness and enjoy your healthy breakfast!

12. Breakfast Smoothie Bowl

Why not start the day with a filling smoothie bowl?

This is a great source of good fats thanks to the avocado and coconut milk.

Preparation time: 10 minutes or less

Cooking time: None

Serves: 1 large bowl (or 2 small bowls)

Ingredients:
- 1 cup creamy coconut milk
- 1/2 soft avocado
- 1/2 vanilla pod or 5 drops vanilla essence
- 1 tbsp. cocoa powder
- 1 tsp. cinnamon (optional)
- Some ice cubes (optional)
- Almonds, strawberry, blueberries or raspberries for topping

Preparation:
1. Add all ingredients into a blender and mix until smooth.

2. Pour the smoothie into a bowl and top with the almonds and fresh berries.

13. High-Protein Hemp Seed Porridge

Hemp seeds are a great source of protein. They are also high in omega 3 and omega 6 fatty acids.

Plus, they add a nutty, slightly sweet touch, and a crunchy texture to your porridge. This makes the perfect breakfast for a cold or rainy day.

Preparation time: 25 minutes

Cooking time: 15 minutes

Serves: 1 large serving

Ingredients:
- 1 cup almond milk
- 1/4 cup hemp seeds (outer shell removed)
- 1 tbsp. flax-seed meal
- 1 tbsp. almond butter
- 1 tsp. cinnamon

For topping:
- Almonds

Preparation:
1. Put the almond milk in a saucepan over low heat and bring to simmer.

2. When simmering, add half of the flax-seed meal, half of the hemp seeds and cinnamon.

3. Stir the mixture and continue to simmer on low heat for 10 minutes while stirring from time to time.

4. Make sure the mixture does not stick to the saucepan.

5. Turn the heat off and add the rest of the ingredients while stirring.

6. Leave to cool down for a couple of minutes.

7. Pour the porridge into a bowl and top with the almonds.

14. Low-Carb Chia and Hemp Seeds Porridge

This is another winter warmer breakfast.

The combination of chia and hemp seeds will boost your energy and provide your body with a good amount of fatty acids.

Preparation time: 5-10 minutes

Cooking time: 10 minutes or less

Serves: 1 large bowl

Ingredients:
- 2 tbsp. black chia seeds
- 2 tbsp. hemp seeds (outer shell removed)
- 1/2 vanilla pod
- 1 tbsp. shredded almonds
- 1/2 cup coconut milk

For topping:
- Handful of blueberries
- 2 large strawberries - sliced

Preparation:
1. Combine all ingredients in a saucepan and mix well.

2. Let the mixture stand for 5 minutes until the chia seeds assume a jelly-like appearance.

3. Put on the stove top at very low heat.

4. Warm up the mixture until bubbles appear.

5. Pour the porridge into a bowl and top with the blueberries and strawberries.

15. Quinoa Breakfast Bowl

With this super-fast breakfast recipe, you will benefit from the excellent properties of quinoa. This very popular health food is gluten-free and very high in protein.

On top of that, quinoa is very nutritious and high in fiber. It is delicious cold, or you can warm it up slightly on the stove or microwave. This great energetic breakfast is the perfect kickstart to a busy day ahead.

Preparation time: 5 minutes

Cooking time: 1 minute

Serves: 1

Ingredients:

- 1/2 cup plain cooked quinoa
- 1/3 cup unsweetened almond milk
- 1 tbsp. almond butter

For topping:

- 1/2 cup fresh blueberries (you can use frozen blueberries as well)
- 1 tsp. cinnamon

Preparation:

1. Combine the quinoa, almond milk and almond butter in a bowl.

2. Mix well together until you have a creamy mixture.

3. Add blueberries for toppings and sprinkle with cinnamon.

4. If you wish to have your breakfast warm, place in the microwave or stove top before topping with berries.

Lunch Recipes

16. Palm Heart Tacos

A lighter, healthier version of tacos. Besides being low-carb, it is perfectly seasoned with well-balanced flavors.

Preparation time: 20 minutes

Cooking time: 5 minutes

Serves: 4

Ingredients:

For the filling:

- 2 14oz. cans palm hearts, rinsed and drained
- 4 tablespoons coconut aminos
- 1 teaspoon chili sauce
- 2 tablespoons olive oil
- 1 teaspoon minced garlic

For the sauce:

- 2 cups hemp seeds
- ½ cup filtered water
- ½ cup fresh lemon juice
- 1 pinch Himalayan salt

For the tacos:

- 1 head lettuce
- ½ cup shredded cabbage
- 1 lime, squeezed

Directions:

1. Make the filling; chop palm hearts into desired pieces.

2. Place the hearts in a bowl along with coconut aminos, chili sauce, and garlic.

3. Cover and refrigerate for 15 minutes.

4. In the meantime, make the hemp seed sauce; place all sauce ingredients into a food blender.

5. Blend until smooth.

6. Heat olive oil in a pan. Add the marinated palm hearts and cook over medium heat for 5 minutes.

7. To assemble; take two lettuce leaves and place in front of you.

8. Add the palm hearts and top with shredded cabbage. Drizzle tacos with hemp seeds sauce and lime juice.

9. Serve immediately.

17. Noodles With Pesto

Sea-vegetable noodles with rich and creamy avocado pesto are the perfect lunch option when you simply need something light and refreshing.

Preparation time: 10 minutes + inactive time

Serves: 4

Ingredients:

- 1 package seaweed noodles/kelp noodles
- 2 cups vegetable stock
- 2 tablespoons coconut aminos

For the pesto:

- ½ cup extra-virgin olive oil
- 1 ½ avocados
- 1 cup baby spinach
- 1 pinch red pepper flakes
- ¼ cup fresh basil
- 2 tablespoons almonds
- 2 cloves garlic
- Sea salt and black pepper to taste

Directions:

1. Combine vegetable stock and coconut aminos in a bowl.

2. Add noodles and soak for 30 minutes.

3. In the meantime, make the pesto by combining all the pesto ingredients in a food blender.

4. Blend until smooth.

5. Drain the noodles and place in a wide bowl.

6. Top with avocado pesto and toss to combine.

7. Serve.

18. "Sausages" With Aioli

Eggplants are a versatile vegetable, and can be used for many dishes. Try this version of eggplant "sausages" with creamy garlic aioli.

An interesting dish with a great nutritional profile!

Preparation time: 10 minutes + inactive time

Cooking time: 8 minutes

Serves: 6

Ingredients:

Sausages:

- 6 long Japanese eggplants
- ¼ cup olive oil
- 1 teaspoon Italian seasoning
- 1 teaspoon ground fennel seeds
- 2 cloves garlic, minced
- 1 ½ teaspoons kosher salt
- Black pepper, to taste
- Cayenne pepper, to taste

Aioli:

- 4 tablespoons extra-virgin olive oil
- 1 cup silvered almonds
- 2 cloves garlic
- 4 tablespoons lemon juice
- ¼ cup filtered water
- Salt and white pepper, to taste

Extras:

- Keto buns of your choosing

Directions:

1. Make the sausages; peel eggplants using a veggie peeler.

2. Place the eggplants in a zip-lock bag with olive oil, spices, and herbs.

3. Refrigerate eggplants for at least 4 hours or overnight.

4. Heat cast-iron grill pan over medium-high heat. Cook marinated eggplants for 3-4 minutes per side.

5. Make the aioli; place aioli ingredients in a food blender. Blend until smooth for 1 minute.

6. Gradually add water until desired texture is reached. Chill for 30 minutes.

7. To assemble; serve "sausages" with keto-friendly buns, topped with aioli sauce.

19. Cauliflower Salad

Salads, cold or warm, are a perfect lunch option. This one is fairly easy to make, loaded with essential nutrients.

Preparation time: 10 minutes + inactive time

Cooking time: 10 minutes

Serves: 4

Ingredients:

Salad:

- 1 medium head cauliflower
- 1 ½ cups sliced mushrooms, oyster or shiitake
- 1 ½ tablespoons olive oil
- 1 teaspoon fresh dill
- 1 teaspoons chopped chives
- ½ teaspoon smoked paprika
- Salt and pepper, to taste

Sauce:

- ½ cup extra-virgin olive oil
- ¼ cup unsweetened soy milk
- 1 teaspoon raw cider vinegar
- Salt and white pepper, to taste

Directions:

1. Make the salad; cut cauliflower into tiny florets.

2. Place the cauliflower florets into a pan and cover with water.

3. Bring to a boil and reduce heat. Simmer for 3-4 minutes or until crisp tender.

4. In the meantime, heat olive oil in a skillet. Cook mushrooms for 5-8 minutes or until soft. Toss in the cauliflower and shake to coat with oil. Season to taste with salt and pepper.

5. Make the sauce; make sure oil and milk are equal temperatures. It is a very important step.

6. Place soy milk, cider vinegar, and seasonings in a food blender. Blend until smooth. While the blender is running low, gradually stream in extra-virgin olive oil.

7. Blend until thickens.

8. In a bowl, toss cauliflower with prepared sauce, dill, and chives.

9. Divide between bowls and sprinkle with paprika. Chill briefly before serving.

20. Spinach Zucchini Boats

Delicate zucchinis filled with spinach and a vegan alternative to milk-made cheese. If you miss the cheesy consistency, this is for you.

Preparation time: 20 minutes

Cooking time: 20 minutes

Serves: 4

Ingredients:

- 4 zucchinis
- 4 tablespoons blanched almond flour
- 4 tablespoons coconut oil
- 4 tablespoons coconut cream
- 1/8 teaspoon guar gum
- 1 pinch nutmeg
- ¾ cup coconut milk
- 2 cups baby spinach
- Kosher salt and white pepper, to taste

"Cheese":

- ¾ cup almonds
- 3 tablespoons nutritional yeast
- ¼ teaspoon garlic powder

Directions:

1. Heat oven to 400F.

2. Trim zucchinis and cut in half by length. Scoop out the seeds.

3. Place the zucchinis on a baking sheet lined with baking paper. Season with salt and pepper.

4. Heat coconut oil in a skillet. Add almond flour and cook until darkened, to the desired color (go with peanut color).

5. Whisk in coconut milk and nutmeg. Simmer 10 seconds. Add guar gum and stir until thickened.

6. Stir in coconut cream, baby spinach and season with salt. Place aside for 5 minutes.

7. Make the cheese; place all ingredients in a food blender.

8. Blend until coarse mixture is formed. Stir in half the cheese into spinach mixture.

9. Stuff the zucchinis with spinach and sprinkle with nut cheese.

10. Bake 15 minutes or until golden.

Serve warm.

21. Stuffed Portabella With Nut Pate

The portabella mushroom is a nutritional powerhouse, and should be incorporated into your diet if possible.

If you're looking for ways to do so, try out this delicious dish; portabellas stuffed with delicate macadamia nut pate!

Preparation time: 10 minutes

Cooking time: 15 minutes

Serves: 4

Ingredients:

- 4 portabella mushrooms caps, stems removed
- 1 tablespoon olive oil
- 1 tablespoon coconut aminos
- Salt and pepper, to taste

Nut pate:

- 1 cup macadamia nuts, soaked 2 hours
- 1 tablespoon coconut aminos
- 1 celery stalk, chopped
- Kosher salt, to taste

Directions:

1. Heat oven to 375F and line a baking sheet with parchment paper.

2. In a bowl, beat olive oil with coconut aminos. Brush in mushroom caps with oil mixture and arrange onto a baking sheet.

3. Bake for 15 minutes.

4. In the meantime, make the nut pate; rinse and drain macadamia nuts. Place the macadamia nuts and celery in a food processor and process until just smooth. In the last seconds of processing, add coconut aminos and salt to taste.

5. Process until the coconut aminos is incorporated.

6. Remove the portabella from the oven and place on a plate. Fill with macadamia pate and serve warm.

22. Savory Crepes With Mushroom Cream

Another tasty portabella option, this time creamy, with a nice touch of garlic.

Preparation time: 15 minutes

Cooking time: 15 minutes

Serves: 4

Crepes:

- 2 tablespoons coconut flour
- 1 1/3 cups almond milk
- 4 tablespoons coconut oil
- 2 tablespoons flax seeds + 2/3 cup water

Mushroom cream:

- 8 portabella mushrooms, caps only
- ¼ cup olive oil
- ½ cup macadamia nuts soaked 4 hours
- 2 sprigs fresh thyme
- 2 tablespoons coconut cream
- 4 cloves garlic, unpeeled
- Salt and white pepper, to taste

Directions:

1. Make the crepes; in a food blender, blend all ingredients.

2. Let the batter rest for 15 minutes.

3. Heat a large non-stick skillet over medium heat. Pour ¼ cup batter into skillet and swirl to distribute the batter evenly over the skillet bottom.

4. Cook until bubbles appear and carefully fill the crepe to another side.

5. Cook for 1 minute. Repeat with remaining batter. Keep pancakes warm.

6. Heat oven to 375F and grease baking sheet with some cooking spray.

7. Place the mushrooms onto a baking sheet and season with salt.

8. In a food blender, process olive oil, garlic, and thyme. Brush each mushroom with prepared mixture and bake for 15 minutes.

9. Transfer the mushrooms to a food blender. Drain and rinse macadamia nuts and place in a food blender with mushrooms. Blend until desired consistency is reached.

10. Spread the pate over crepes and roll or fold gently.

23. Crust-Less Quiche

A wonderful combination of asparagus, kale, and a nut-based creamy filling — all combined in a crust-less quiche.

Preparation time: 15 minutes

Cooking time: 30 minutes

Serves: 4-6

Ingredients:

- 4 tablespoons coconut oil
- 2 cups asparagus, trimmed and chopped
- 2 cups kale
- 8oz. sliced oyster mushrooms
- 1 garlic clove, minced
- Salt and pepper, to taste

Filling:

- 1 cup Brazil nuts, soaked 4 hours
- ¼ cup nutritional yeast
- 1 ¾ cup full-fat coconut milk
- 1/3 cup softened coconut butter
- ½ cup almond flour
- 3 tablespoons lemon juice
- 1 teaspoon turmeric powder
- Salt and pepper, to taste

Directions:

1. Heat coconut oil in a skillet. Add sliced mushrooms, minced garlic, and cook 6 minutes.

2. Toss in kale and asparagus and cook 3-4 minutes, Season to taste.

3. Remove from heat and place aside.

4. Make the filling; rinse and drain Brazil nuts. Place in a food processor with coconut milk and process until creamy.

5. Add remaining ingredients and process until smooth.

6. Transfer into a bowl, and stir in kale-mushroom mixture.

7. Heat oven to 350F. Pour mixture into 9-inch pie pan and bake 30 minutes or until firm to the touch.

8. Cool 20 minutes before slicing and serving.

24. Veggie Fritters With Avocado

Fritters are not reserved only for breakfast.

These will satisfy even the most demanding gourmet lover.

Preparation time: 10 minutes

Cooking time: 10 minutes

Serves: 4

Ingredients:

- 1 large zucchini
- 2 portabella mushrooms
- 1 tablespoon ground flax seeds + 3 tablespoons water
- ¼ cup almond meal
- 1 cup packed chopped spinach
- 1 avocado
- ¼ cup macadamia nuts soaked 4 hours
- 1 tablespoon raw hemp seeds
- 1 teaspoon dried basil
- Salt and pepper, to taste
- 2-3 tablespoons olive oil, for frying

Sauce:

- ½ cup silvered almonds, soaked 4 hours
- 3 tablespoons extra-virgin olive oil
- 1 clove garlic
- ½ teaspoon chili powder
- ¼ cup filtered water
- 2 tablespoons lemon juice
- Salt, to taste

Directions:

1. Make the fritters; combine flax seeds and water in a small bowl. Place aside for 10 minutes.

2. Shred zucchinis and mushrooms. Squeeze to remove excess liquid and place in a bowl.

3. Rinse and drain macadamia and process in a food blender with hemp seeds until creamy.

4. Add the macadamia cream and flax mixture into a bowl with zucchinis.

5. Add the chopped spinach and stir to combine.

6. Heat half the oil in a pan. Scoop fritters into the pan and cook 2 minutes per side.

7. Repeat with remaining oil and batter.

8. Make sauce; drain and rinse soaked almonds. Place in a food blender with remaining ingredients, except extra-virgin olive oil. Blend until smooth. While the blender is running low, stream in the olive oil and blend until emulsified.

9. Serve fritters with sauce.

25. Creamy Cauliflower Soup

A rich, creamy, and aromatic soup. Super healthy, and very easy to make.

Preparation time: 10 minutes

Cooking time: 15 minutes

Serves: 4

Ingredients:

- 2 cups cauliflower florets
- 2 cups sliced wild mushrooms
- 2 cups full-fat coconut milk
- 2 tablespoons avocado oil
- 1 teaspoon dried celery flakes
- ½ tablespoons fresh chopped thyme
- 1 clove garlic, minced
- Salt and pepper, to taste

Directions:

1. In a saucepan, combine cauliflower, coconut milk, and celery flakes.

2. Cover and bring to a boil over medium-high heat.

3. Reduce heat and simmer for 6-7 minutes. Remove from the heat and puree using an immersion blender.

4. In the meantime, heat avocado oil in a skillet. Add garlic and thyme and cook until fragrant. Toss in wild mushrooms and cook for 6-7 minutes or until tender.

5. Pour in pureed cauliflower and bring to a boil. Reduce heat and simmer 6-8 minutes or until thickened.

6. Serve warm with Keto bread.

26. Curry Cauliflower Rice

This recipe can sound a little bit misleading, since rice should not be part of a low carb diet.

However, there isn't actually any rice in this recipe. Cauliflower is what gives this dish a texture similar to rice, while still keeping the carbs very low.

Preparation time: 10 minutes

Cooking time: 10 minutes

Serves: 4

Ingredients:

- 1 head cauliflower
- 1 clove of garlic - chopped
- 1 tbsp. coconut cream
- 2 tbsp. extra virgin olive oil
- 1 tbsp. mild curry powder
- 1/8 tsp. cinnamon
- ½ cup cashew nuts - halved
- ½ tsp. salt
- Black pepper to taste
- ½ cup coriander – roughly chopped
- Juice of ½ lemon

Preparation:

1. Separate the cauliflower florets from the stem.

2. Chop the florets into approximately 2-inch pieces.

3. Place half of the cauliflower into a food processor. Pulse with 1 second intervals until the cauliflower pieces look like grains of rice.

4. Move the processed cauliflower into a bowl.

5. Repeat the process with the other half of cauliflower.

6. Heat the extra virgin olive oil in a large saucepan over a medium heat.

7. When the oil is hot, add the curry powder, cinnamon, and fry for approximately 1 minute.

8. Add the cauliflower and cashew nuts and stir until coated with the curry powder

9. Add salt and coconut cream and cook for 5-8 minutes or until tender.

10. Remove from the heat; add coriander, black pepper and lemon juice.

11. Let it rest for couple minutes and serve.

27. Zucchini Noodles with Vegan Cheese Sauce

This easy-to-make zucchini recipe will satisfy your cravings for a cheesy sauce, and will give your body a good dose of healthy fats thanks to the extra virgin olive oil.

Preparation time: 15 minutes

Serves: 2

Ingredients:

- 3 medium zucchini – sliced very thin with a mandolin slicer or basic grater
- ½ cup walnuts – chopped
- Black pepper

For the Cheesy Sauce:

- 2 tbsp. extra virgin olive oil
- Juice of 1 small lemon
- 2 tbsp. nutritional yeast
- Pinch of salt

Preparation:

1. Combine all ingredients for the cheesy sauce and mix together.

2. Place the zucchini noodles and walnuts into a bowl.

3. Pour the cheesy sauce onto the zucchini noodles and top with ground black pepper. Toss gently and serve.

28. Asian-Style Green Beans with Walnut Butter

This incredibly quick and simple recipe combines the high fat of the walnut butter and coconut oil with the low-carb green beans.

This dish can be enjoyed on its own as a quick lunch or served as a side.

Preparation time: 10 minutes

Cooking time: 10 minutes

Serves: 3-4

Ingredients:

- 1 ½ lb. green beans – trimmed
- 2 tbsp. walnut butter
- 2 tbsp. tamari
- 2 tbsp. avocado oil
- 1 tbsp. water
- 1 tbsp. coconut oil
- 1 clove of garlic – minced
- 1 tsp. fresh ginger – minced
- ½ tsp crushed black pepper

Preparation:

1. Steam the green beans for approximately 5 minutes or until just tender.

2. Rinse under very cold water, drain and set aside.

3. In a small ball mix together the walnut butter, tamari, avocado oil and water and set aside.

4. Heat the coconut oil in a large wok or frying pan over a medium-high heat.

5. Add the beans and stir-fry for 30-40 seconds.

6. Remove the beans from the pan or wok and set aside.

7. In the same wok used for the beans, add the garlic, ginger and crushed black pepper.

8. Stir-fry for 15 seconds.

9. Add the beans to the wok and sir-fry again for 30 seconds.

10. Add the walnut mixture previously prepared and stir-fry until the beans are all coated with the mixture.

11. Serve immediately.

29. Colourful Walnut Tacos

These tacos are a great alternative to regular meat-filled ones. The walnuts mixed with the rest of the ingredients will give a meat-like texture packed with proteins.

The corn flour tortillas are replaced by lettuce leaves as a low-carb option.

Preparation time: 15 minutes

Soaking time: Overnight

Serves: 2

Ingredients:

For the Tacos:

- 2 cups walnuts – soaked overnight
- 2 tbsp. ground cumin
- 1 tbsp. extra virgin olive oil
- 1 tsp. paprika
- Salt
- ¼ tsp. cayenne pepper
- Lettuce leaves as many as needed

For the Guacamole:

- 1 large soft avocado or 2 small
- Juice of 2 limes
- Salt & Pepper

For the Pico de Gallo:

- 2 large tomatoes – chopped in very small square pieces
- ¼ red onion – chopped in very small square pieces
- Juice of 2 limes
- Salt & Pepper
- 1 tsp. extra virgin olive oil
- ½ cup coriander – roughly chopped

Preparation:

1. Soak the walnuts overnight.

2. Put all ingredients for the tacos, except for the lettuce leaves, in a food processor.

3. Process until the mixture looks like the texture of minced meat.

4. Set aside.

5. In a small ball place the avocado, salt and pepper, and lemon juice and mash until smooth.

6. In another bowl, place the ingredients for the Pico de Gallo and mix well together.

7. Scoop the taco mix into the lettuce leaves and serve with guacamole and Pico de Gallo on the side.

30. Sautéed Brussel Sprouts with Radicchio and Almonds

Here we have another favorite with Brussel sprouts. This time, we paired it with radicchio.

Radicchio is a great source of vitamins B, C and K, and is high in antioxidants.

Preparation time: 10 minutes

Cooking time: 20-25 minutes

Serves: 3-4

Ingredients:

- 1 ½ lb. Brussel sprouts – stem removed and sliced in half
- 2 heads Radicchio – roughly chopped
- 3 tbsp. avocado oil
- ¼ cup Almonds – shaved
- ¼ cup of red onion – diced
- 2 cloves of garlic – minced
- Salt & Pepper

Preparation:

1. Heat 2 tablespoons of avocado oil in a large frying pan or wok over medium-high heat.

2. Add the Brussel sprouts and cook them for about 10 minutes. Stir occasionally.

3. In the meantime, heat the remaining avocado oil in a small frying pan over medium heat.

4. Add the red onion and sauté for 4-5 minutes until translucent.

5. Add the almonds and garlic.

6. Cook for an additional 4-5 minutes until they become lightly brown. Remove from the heat as you do not want them to burn.

7. Back to the sprouts. When they start to brown, add the Radicchio and continue to cook until the Radicchio becomes tender.

8. Remove from the heat and add the toasted almond mixture.

9. Add salt and pepper, toss everything gently and serve while still hot.

31. Almond & Coconut Asparagus

Asparagus are some of the most delicious veggies around, and they can go well with a wide range of other ingredients.

The bright green part of the asparagus is packed with vitamins, minerals and fiber to help your body stay healthy.

Preparation time: 10 minutes

Cooking time: 15 minutes

Serves: 4

Ingredients:

- 1 ½ lb. asparagus – remove the white part at the back
- 1 tbsp. coconut oil
- ½ cup white onion – diced
- 1 clove of garlic - chopped
- 2 tbsp. sliced almonds
- 1 tsp. paprika
- ½ tsp. red chili flakes
- Pinch of salt
- 1 cup coconut milk
- Juice of 1 lime
- ½ cup fresh coriander – roughly chopped

Preparation:

1. Heat the oil in a large frying pan over medium heat.

2. Add the almonds and fry until they become to brown. Be careful not to burn them.

3. Move the almonds to a plate and set aside.

4. Return the empty pan to the heat; add onion, garlic, paprika, chili flakes and a pinch of salt.

5. Cook until the onion becomes soft and stats to brown.

6. Add the coconut milk and stir well.

7. Add the asparagus and stir well.

8. Bring to the boil, cover and reduce heat to low.

9. Simmer until the asparagus are tender, approximately 5 minutes. If you like the asparagus softer let them simmer for longer.

10. When you are happy with the tenderness of the asparagus, remove the lid and continue cooking until the sauce becomes a little thicker. If you like it runnier, you can remove from heat now.

11. Once removed from heat, add lime juice and coriander. Stir once more and serve.

32. Sautéed Quick Lunch Veggies

This mix of tasty veggies is one of the quickest and easiest recipes to prepare. In 30 minutes, you will have a delicious and healthy lunch full of protein and good fats.

You will feel full, energetic and ready for the second part of your day.

Preparation time: 15 minutes

Cooking time: 15 minutes

Serves: 2

Ingredients:

- 2 tbsp. extra virgin olive oil
- ½ small red onion – finely chopped
- 1 green pepper – diced
- 2 cups broccoli florets – cut into small pieces
- 2 cups cauliflower florets – cut into small pieces
- 2 cups spinach – roughly chopped
- 1 cup mushrooms – chopped
- 2 cloves of garlic – finely chopped
- 1 cup Brussels sprouts – stems cut off and cut into quarters
- Salt & Pepper
- ½ cup fresh parsley – roughly chopped

Preparation:

1. Heat the oil over medium heat in a large frying pan.

2. Add the onions and cook until translucent.

3. Add the garlic and cook for another 2 minutes approximately.

4. Add all your vegetables except for the spinach and sauté for approximately 10 minutes. Stir occasionally.

5. Add the spinach, salt and pepper.

6. Stir well together and cook for another 5 minutes. If you like your vegetables softer, cook for extra 10 minutes in total.

7. Take off the heat and add fresh parsley.

8. Serve immediately.

33. Cucumber Salad

In the culinary world, cucumbers are a versatile choice — you can pair them with almost anything. For this particular recipe, we combined it with avocado and nuts for that extra fatty kick.

You can make a large portion and have it as a light lunch, or divide it into smaller portions for a delicious side dish.

Preparation time: 15 minutes

Serves: 4

Ingredients:

- 2 large cucumbers - peeled, deseeded and cut into julienne
- 1 cup cherry tomatoes - cut into quarters
- 1 small soft avocado - sliced
- 1 clove of garlic - minced
- 1/2 cup olives - chopped
- 1/2 cup walnuts - chopped

For the Dressing:

- 2 tbsp. extra virgin olive oil
- 1 tsp. grainy mustard
- Juice of 2 lemons
- 1/2 tsp. salt
- 1 tsp. freshly ground black pepper
- 1/4 cup fresh parsley - roughly chopped

Preparation:

1. In a large bowl combine the cucumber, cherry tomatoes, avocado, walnuts, olives and minced garlic.

2. In a small bowl put the lemon juice, mustard, salt, and pepper. Whisk together.

3. Slowly add olive oil while whisking. Keep whisking until obtaining a creamy dressing. If the dressing is too thick, you can add more olive oil or few drops of water.

4. Pour dressing onto salad and gently toss together. Serve and enjoy.

34. Cauliflower Summer Salad

This is another low-carb salad to add freshness and taste to your hot summer days.

We added nuts for a better protein intake, and extra virgin olive oil for a fat boost.

Preparation time: 15 minutes

Serves: 5

Ingredients:

- 1/2 head of iceberg lettuce - thinly sliced
- 3.5 oz. cauliflower florets - raw and cut into small pieces
- 1 medium carrot - cut into julienne strips
- 1 cup button mushrooms - peeled and thinly sliced
- 1 cup cherry tomatoes - halved
- 2 oz. fennel - thinly sliced
- 1/2 cup macadamia nuts - crushed

For the Dressing:

- 2 tbsp. extra virgin olive oil
- Juice of 1 lemon
- 1 tsp. balsamic vinegar
- Salt and Pepper to taste

Preparation:

1. Combine all the vegetables in a large bowl.

2. In a separate small bowl whisk in together all ingredients for the dressing.

3. Pour the dressing onto the salad, toss gently until evenly coated and serve.

35. Fennel and Green Beans Pesto Salad

Some vegetables are better eaten raw. As an added bonus, raw food is quick and easy to make, saving you time for other things.

Preparation time: 15 minutes

Serves: 3

Ingredients:

- 1 lb. green beans - chopped into medium pieces
- 2 fennels - outer removed and thinly sliced
- 1 large tomato - diced
- 1/2 cup cashew nuts - chopped

For Pesto:

- 2 cups basil leaves
- 2 tbsp. extra virgin olive oil
- 1 clove garlic -
- 1 tbsp. lemon juicc
- Salt & Pepper to taste

Preparation:

1. Prepare pesto first.

2. Put the basil and garlic in a food processor or blender.

3. Process or blend until the basil and garlic are completely chopped.

4. Add the olive oil in a stream while the processor or blender is running.

5. Add the lemon juice, salt, and pepper and mix again. At this point, you should have a nice smooth runny paste. Taste your pesto and adjust for salt and pepper if necessary.

6. Take a large bowl and add all the salad ingredients.

7. Pour the pesto over the salad and gently toss to combine.

8. Your salad is ready to serve.

36. Baby Spinach, Mushrooms and Nuts Salad

If you love salads, but are a bit bored of using lettuce, baby spinach is a great alternative.

The young, crunchy leaves are a great source of iron. Pair it with the avocado dressing and nuts, and you will have a delicious low-carb, high fat salad ready to serve.

Preparation time: 15 minutes

Cooking time: 10 minutes

Serves: 2

Ingredients:

- 2 cups of baby spinach – roughly chopped
- 1 cup button mushrooms – sliced
- 1 cup cherry tomatoes – halved
- 1 clove of garlic – chopped
- 1 tbsp. extra virgin olive oil
- Salt & Pepper to taste
- 2 tbsp. water
- ½ cup of walnuts – roughly chopped

For the Dressing:

- ½ soft avocado
- 2 tbsp. extra virgin olive oil
- Juice of 1 large lemon
- Salt & Pepper to taste

Preparation:

1. Put the oil in a frying pan and preheat over a medium-high heat.

2. When the oil is hot, throw in the garlic and cook for 1 minute.

3. Add the mushrooms, salt and pepper and cook until the mushrooms release their water and become small.

4. Add water and keep cooking for another minute.

5. Set aside and leave it to cool down. Drain the mushrooms and keep the cooking juice.

6. In a large bowl, place the baby spinach, cherry tomatoes and walnuts.

7. Put the avocado, olive oil, lemon juice, salt and pepper in a blender. Blend for about 30 seconds until you have a smooth and creamy dressing. If the dressing is too thick you can add some drops of water and blend again.

8. Taste and adjust for salt and pepper if necessary.

9. Pour the dressing onto the salad and gently toss before serving.

37. Roasted Vegetables, Tofu & Pumpkin Seeds Salad

For this one, we have combined a choice of low-carb vegetables with fats from olives, and we have added the extra proteins of pumpkin seeds and tofu.

Everything combined together makes this salad a perfect filling choice for a light lunch or dinner, packed with all the right nutrients.

Preparation time: 10 minutes

Cooking time: 40 minutes

Serves: 4

Ingredients:

- 1 pack extra firm tofu – cut into bite size cubes approximately 1" size
- ½ head of broccoli – cut florets into approximately 2" size, discard the stems
- ½ head cauliflower – cut florets into approximately 1" size, discard the stems
- 1 cup white button mushrooms – halved
- 1 eggplant – cut into approximately 2" chunks
- Extra virgin olive oil
- ¼ cup black olives – chopped
- ¼ cup pumpkin seeds
- Salt & Pepper to taste

Preparation:

1. Preheat oven to 400F.

2. Drain the tofu and pat with a paper towel to absorb as much water as possible.

3. Cut tofu into cubes.

4. Drizzle 1 tablespoon of extra virgin olive oil on a baking tray. Place the tofu on the baking tray and shake gently so that the tofu gets evenly coated with oil.

5. When the oven reaches temperature, place the tofu on the upper rack and start roasting.

6. Place all the pre-cut vegetable on another baking tray, add 2 tablespoons of extra virgin olive oil, a pinch of salt and freshly ground black pepper and toss gently to evenly coat.

7. Place the baking tray in the oven on the lower rack.

8. Roast for approximately 30 minutes, checking the vegetables from time to time.

9. Remove vegetables from the oven and set aside to cool.

10. If some of the vegetables are not completely cooked, remove the cooked through vegetable and leave the rest in the oven.

11. Take the tofu out of the oven and flip over on the tray.

12. Turn up the oven to 450F.

13. Place the tofu back in the oven and roast for another 10-15 minutes. Make sure the tofu gets a nice brown colour on both sides.

14. The tofu should be brown and crispy on the outside and soft on the inside.

15. Remove from oven and let it cool down for approximately 5 minutes.

16. Add the pumpkin seeds, olives and tofu to the roasted vegetables.

17. As an option you can add some fresh parsley and lemon juice.

18. Gently toss together and serve.

38. Kale, Avocado & Grilled Tempeh Salad

Tempeh is an excellent source of vegan protein that originates from Indonesia. It is very healthy, while also being versatile; you can have it deep fried, pan fried, grilled, steamed, and so on.

It is delicious in soups and curries, in particular. For this recipe, we paired it with raw kale for that extra crunch.

Preparation time: 10 minutes

Cooking time: 10 minutes

Serves: 4

Ingredients:

- 8 oz. pack of tempeh – cut into slices approximately 0.2" thick
- 1 tbsp. coconut oil
- 8 oz. black kale – rib removed from each stalk
- 4 oz. radishes – very thinly sliced
- 1 cup cherry tomatoes - halved
- 1 soft avocado - diced

For the Dressing:

- 3 tbsp. extra virgin olive oil
- 1 tsp. Dijon mustard
- Juice of 2 lemons
- 1 tsp. apple cider vinegar
- Salt & Pepper to taste

Preparation:

1. Preheat grill to medium-high.

2. Oil the grill rack using the coconut oil.

3. Place tempeh on the rack and grill until lightly charred, approximately 3-5 minutes each side.

4. Set tempeh aside.

5. Stack the kale leaves in small batches and cut into thin slices.

6. In a large salad bowl, place the kale, radishes, avocado and cherry tomatoes.

7. Crumble the grilled tempeh over the top.

8. In a small bowl, whisk dressing ingredients together until creamy.

9. Pour the dressing over the salad, toss gently and serve.

Dinner Recipes

39. Keto Vegan Falafel

Falafel is usually made with chickpeas or fava beans. However, since we're shooting for low-carb, we chose some other fitting ingredients.

If you love a classic falafel, try this.

Preparation time: 10 minutes

Cooking time: 10 minutes

Serves: 4-5

Ingredients:

- ½ cup raw hemp hearts
- 1 tablespoon chopped cilantro
- 1 tablespoon chopped basil
- 2 cloves garlic, minced
- ½ teaspoon ground cumin seeds
- ½ teaspoon chili powder
- 1 tablespoon flax meal + 2 tablespoons filtered water
- Sea salt and pepper, to taste
- Avocado or coconut oil, to fry

Sauce:

- ½ cup tahini
- ¼ cup fresh lime juice
- ½ cup filtered water
- 2 tablespoons extra-virgin olive oil
- Sea salt, to taste
- A good pinch ground cumin seeds

Directions:

1. Mix flax with filtered water in a small bowl.

2. Place aside for 10 minutes.

3. In meantime, combine raw hemp hearts, cilantro, basil, garlic, cumin, chili, and seasonings in a food processor.

4. Process until just comes together. Add the flax seeds mixture and process until finely blended and uniform.

5. Heat approximately 2 tablespoons avocado oil in a skillet. Shape 1 tablespoon mixture into balls and fry for 3-4 minutes or until deep golden brown.

6. Remove from the skillet and place on a plate lined with paper towels.

7. Make the sauce; combine all ingredients in a food blender. Blend until smooth and creamy.

8. Serve falafel with fresh lettuce salad and tahini sauce.

40. Italian Baked Mushrooms

Delicious tender mushrooms made with Italian herbs, extra-virgin olive oil, and some super-fast creamy nut cheese.

Preparation time: 10 minutes

Cooking time: 25 minutes

Serves: 4

Ingredients:

- 1lb. sliced portabella mushrooms, caps only
- 4 green bell peppers, sliced
- 4 tablespoons olive oil
- 1 tablespoon extra-virgin olive oil
- 2 tablespoons fresh chopped basil
- 1 teaspoon dried oregano
- Salt and pepper, to taste

Topping:

- 1 cup macadamia nuts
- 4 tablespoons nutritional yeast
- ½ teaspoon dried garlic
- Salt, to taste

Directions:

1. Heat oven to 400F.

2. Cut bell peppers in half, remove seeds and place on a baking sheet. Drizzle the peppers with 1 tablespoon olive oil and sprinkle with black pepper.

3. Roast 25 minutes or until slightly charred. Transfer into the clean zip-lock bag and allow to cool completely. Peel off the skin and place the peppers with some salt, extra-virgin olive oil, and basil in a food blender.

4. Blend until smooth.

5. Heat remaining olive oil in a skillet. Add oregano and cook until fragrant. Toss in the mushrooms and cook for 8 minutes.

6. Make the topping; in a food processor process, the topping ingredients until a fine meal is formed.

7. Transfer the mushrooms into baking dish. Top with green bell pepper sauce and macadamia nut topping.

8. Bake 20 minutes in the heated oven at 400F.

9. Serve warm.

41. Avocado & Spinach Gazpacho

Cold gazpacho soup you can make in advance and serve whenever you want.

It is a perfect option for a summer dinner, and is best served with some keto-friendly bread croutons.

Preparation time: 10 minutes

Serves: 4-6

Ingredients:

- 1 ½ avocado, peeled, chopped
- 2 medium cucumbers, peeled and chopped
- 1 handful baby spinach
- 2 stalks celery
- 2 tablespoons extra-virgin olive oil
- ½ jalapeno pepper, seeded
- 2 cup cold homemade vegetable stock or water
- 1/3 cup loosely packed cilantro
- 2 cloves garlic, minced
- 2 limes, juiced
- 1 teaspoon ground fennel seeds
- Sea salt and pepper, to taste

Directions:

1. In a food processor, process cucumbers and celery, and place in a large bowl (you can also use a food blender).

2. Process celery, jalapeno and garlic, and place in a bowl.

3. Next, process spinach and basil, and place in a bowl.

4. Pour in 2 cups water or vegetable stock and process until smooth. Pour into a bowl, reserving 2 cups mixture.

5. Add in remaining ingredients and process until smooth. Pour into a bowl, and stir to combine.

6. Chill for few hours before serving.

42. Healthy Green Tabbouleh

This Ketogenic version of well-known Eastern salad will surprise you with its easy preparation and outstanding flavors.

Preparation time: 10 minutes

Cooking time: 5 minutes

Serves: 4

Ingredients:

- 3 cups "riced" cauliflower
- 3 tablespoons extra-virgin coconut oil
- 1 avocado, peeled, cubed
- 2 large cucumber, peeled and diced
- 3 cups spinach, chopped
- ½ cup fresh lemon juice
- ½ cup extra-virgin olive oil
- ½ cup fresh chopped parsley
- ½ cup fresh chopped mint
- 1 clove garlic, minced
- 1 spring onion (optional) chopped
- Salt and pepper, to taste

Directions:

1. Heat coconut oil in a skillet.

2. Add cauliflower and cook over medium heat for 5 minutes or until crisp tender.

3. Remove from heat and place aside.

4. Prepare the remaining ingredients, as described.

5. Place the chopped vegetables in a bowl. Top with chopped herbs and cauliflower.

6. In a small bowl, whisk lemon juice, olive oil, and minced garlic.

7. Pour over tabbouleh and toss to combine.

8. Chill briefly before serving.

43. Olive Cauliflower Non-Meatballs

Vegetable "meatballs" are often not the healthiest option, as they sacrifice nutrition in order to resemble actual meat as closely as possible.

However, these little beauties, made largely from cauliflower, are loaded with quality ingredients that your body will appreciate.

Preparation time: 10 minutes

Cooking time: 25 minutes

Serves: 4

Ingredients:

- 2 cups cauliflower florets
- ½ cup sprouted mung beans
- 1 tablespoon ground flax seeds
- 2 tablespoons extra-virgin coconut oil
- ½ cup chopped green olives
- 1 clove garlic, minced
- ¼ cup chopped fresh parsley
- ½ teaspoon red chili flakes
- 1 teaspoon dried oregano
- Salt and pepper, to taste

Chutney:

- ¼ cup mint
- ¼ cup coriander
- ½ juiced lemon
- 1 green chili
- ½ cup unsweetened grated coconut
- Salt, to taste

Directions:

1. Place the sprouted mung beans in a pan. Cover with water and simmer for 25-30 minutes.

2. In the last 5 minutes of cooking toss in the cauliflower florets and cook until crisp tender.

3. Place in a colander to drain completely.

4. Transfer in a food blender and blend until smooth.

5. Add olives, garlic, parsley, chili flakes, oregano, salt, and pepper. Combine flax seeds with 2 tablespoons water and place aside to gel.

6. Stir the "flax egg" into the cauliflower mixture and stir all to combine.

7. Shape the mixture into 1 ½ -inch balls and arrange on baking sheet lined with parchment paper.

8. Bake 20 minutes, flip and cook for 5 minutes more.

9. Make the chutney: place all ingredients in a food processor. Process until smooth.

10. Serve meatballs with chutney.

44. Veggie Pizza Deluxe

A vegan, ketogenic pizza? Yes, it's real. This pizza is made with spinach pesto, and topped with some healthy veggies.

You can choose your own topping ingredients to suit your personal tastes, of course.

Preparation time: 15 minutes

Cooking time: 15 minutes

Serves: 6

Ingredients:

Crust:

- 1 cup almond flour
- ¼ cup sifted coconut flour
- 1 teaspoon kosher salt
- ¾ cup ground flax seeds
- 2 tablespoons ground white chia seeds
- 1 tablespoon psyllium husks powder
- 1 cup water

Pesto:

- ½ cup macadamia nuts
- 1 cup baby spinach
- 1 clove garlic
- ½ cup nutritional yeast
- ½ cup avocado oil
- 2 tablespoons lemon juice
- Salt, to taste

Topping:

- 2 tablespoons olive oil
- 1 cup baby Bella mushrooms, sliced
- 1 green bell pepper, sliced
- ½ cup broccoli florets
- Fresh basil, chopped

Directions:

1. Make the crust; combine all crust ingredients in a bowl.

2. Knead until smooth. Cover and place aside for 20 minutes.

3. Roll the dough between two pieces of baking paper to ¼-inch thick. With fingers roll the ends to create a rim that will hold pesto. Transfer the pizza onto a baking sheet lined with parchment paper and bake 10 minutes at 375F.

4. Make the pesto; in a food blender, combine pesto ingredients. Blend until smooth.

5. Make the topping; heat oven to 400F. Spread bell pepper and broccoli onto a baking sheet. Drizzle with oil and season to taste. Roast 10 minutes.

6. Assemble pizza; spread pesto over pizza crust. Top with roasted veggies and mushrooms. Bake 5-6 minutes at 375F. Serve warm.

45. Creamy "Cauli Rice" With Spinach

Sauteed spinach with rice makes a light, healthy, and delicious dinner meal.

Preparation time: 5 minutes

Cooking time: 7 minutes

Serves: 4

Ingredients:

- 3 cups "riced" cauliflower
- 1 ½ cups packed baby spinach
- 1 tablespoon avocado oil
- 2 tablespoons coconut aminos
- 1 teaspoon dried garlic
- ¼ cup macadamia nuts, soaked 4 hours
- 1 tablespoon nutritional yeast
- Salt, to taste

Directions:

1. Heat avocado oil in a skillet.

2. Add cauliflower and cook 3-4 minutes, stirring. Stir in coconut aminos.

3. In the meantime, rinse macadamia and place in a food blender along with garlic and nutritional yeast.

4. Add spinach to cauliflower and cook until wilted.

5. Pour over macadamia mix and cook for 5 minutes. Serve.

46. Eggplant & Zucchini Stack

Zucchini fritters with eggplants as low-carb buns, combined with a creamy avocado sour cream.

Preparation time: 10 minutes

Cooking time: 10 minutes

Serves: 4

Ingredients:

Zucchini fritters:
- 2 cups grated zucchinis
- ¼ cup fresh parsley, chopped
- 2 tablespoons coconut flour
- 1 tablespoon ground flax seeds + 2 tablespoons water
- 1 tablespoon coconut oil
- Salt and pepper, to taste

Eggplant:
- 1 large eggplant, sliced into ¼- inch thick round
- 1 tablespoon coconut oil

Avocado cream:
- 1 avocado, pitted, peeled
- ¼ cup full-fat coconut milk
- 2 tablespoons extra-virgin olive or coconut oil
- 1 tablespoon fresh lime juice
- Salt, to taste

Directions:

1. Make the fritters; place grated zucchinis in a colander and sprinkle with some salt. Leave to drain 10 minutes. Squeeze out liquid as much as possible.

2. In a bowl, combine flax seeds and water. Place aside until gel.

3. Stir in the zucchinis and remaining fritter ingredients, except oil. Heat oil in a skillet.

4. Shape 2 tablespoons zucchini mixture into balls and flatten each gently.

5. Fry the fritters for 3 minutes per side.

6. Prepare the eggplant; season sliced eggplant with salt and place in a colander for 30 minutes. Rinse and pat-dry. Heat grill pan over medium-high heat. Add oil and once hot, grill the eggplant for 3 minutes per side. Place aside and keep warm.

7. Make the sauce; in a food blender, combine all sauce ingredients. Blend until smooth and creamy.

8. To serve; place an eggplant slice in front of you. Top with avocado sauce and sandwich with remaining eggplant slices. You can also add some salad. Serve.

47. Eggplant Fingers With Macadamia Hummus

Crispy, tasty eggplant fingers served with macadamia-based hummus.

This is a perfect dish to serve for dinner parties.

Preparation time: 10 minutes

Cooking time: 45 minutes

Serves: 4

Ingredients:

Eggplant bites:
- 1 medium diced eggplant
- 4 cloves garlic, unpeeled
- 1 tablespoon extra-virgin avocado oil
- 1 cup fine almond flour
- 1 tablespoon flax seeds + 2 tablespoons water
- 1 teaspoon dried basil

Hummus:
- ½ cup macadamia nuts
- 1 clove garlic
- 1 tablespoon water
- 1 tablespoon tahini
- 1 tablespoon coconut oil
- 1 ½ tablespoons fresh lemon juice
- Salt and pepper, to taste

Directions:

1. Make the fingers; combine flax seeds with water in a bowl. Place aside for 10 minutes.

2. Heat oven to 400F and line baking tray with parchment paper.

3. Place eggplants and garlic onto a baking tray and toss with olive oil, salt, and pepper.

4. Roast for 40 minutes. Remove and place aside to cool.

5. Transfer cooled eggplant into a food processor and squeeze garlic from the peel. Add remaining ingredients, including flax seeds and pulse until just combined.

6. Shape the mixture into fingers and arrange on a baking sheet lined with parchment paper.

7. Bake the fingers for 45 minutes, turning halfway through baking.

8. Make the hummus; combine the hummus ingredients in a food processor. Process until smooth.

9. Serve hummus with eggplant fingers.

48. Tofu Salad

Sometimes, you just want to try something different, and this salad is all about new and exciting flavors; marinated tofu served with Bok Choy and chili sambal dressing!

Preparation time: 15 minutes

Cooking time: 30 minutes

Serves: 4

Ingredients:

- 15oz. extra firm drained tofu
- 1 tablespoon coconut aminos
- 1 tablespoon coconut oil
- 2 teaspoons minced garlic
- 1 tablespoon filtered water
- ½ lemon juice

For the salad:

- 9oz. fresh Bok Choy
- 3 tablespoons extra-virgin coconut oil
- 2 tablespoons coconut aminos
- 2 tablespoons chopped parsley
- 1 tablespoon almond butter
- 1 tablespoon ground chili sambal

Directions:

1. Make the tofu; cut tofu into squares and place in a bowl.

2. In a small bowl, whisk coconut aminos, coconut oil, garlic, water, and lemon juice. Pour mixture over tofu and toss gently to combine. Cover and refrigerate 1 hour.

3. Heat oven to 350F and line a baking sheet with parchment paper. Arrange the tofu on a baking sheet and bake 30 minutes.

4. Make the Bok choy; in a bowl, combine all ingredients except Bok choy and lemon juice.

5. Just before tofu is baked, stir in lemon juice. Chop the Bok choy and stir into prepared dressing.

6. Remove tofu cubes from oven and serve with Bok choy.

49. Cauliflower and Cashew Nuts Indian Style

Cauliflower is a very popular veggie among chefs, because of its great versatile texture and because of its ability to absorb other flavors. Cashew nuts add proteins and fat to this exotic flavorsome dish.

Preparation time: 15 minutes

Cooking time: 35 minutes

Serves: 3

Ingredients:

- 1 very large cauliflower – florets and stems chopped into medium pieces
- 3 tbsp. coconut oil
- 1 tsp. cumin seeds
- 1 small handful curry leaves
- ½ tsp. fennel seeds
- 4 cardamom pods
- ½ white onion - fincly chopped
- 5 cloves of garlic – minced
- 1 inch piece of ginger – minced
- 2 medium tomatoes –chopped
- ½ cup Cashew nuts
- 1 tbsp. coriander powder
- ½ tsp. turmeric powder
- ½ tsp. Garam Masala
- ½ cup coconut cream
- ¼ cup of water
- Fresh Coriander – roughly chopped
- Salt & Pepper

Preparation:

1. Heat the coconut oil in a large pot over medium heat.

2. Add cardamom pods, cumin and fennel seeds.

3. When the seeds start splattering add the onion and curry leaves.

4. Fry for a couple of minutes then add a pinch of salt, stir and keep cooking until the onion is translucent (approximately 5 minutes).

5. Add ginger and garlic and cook for another 2-3 minutes.

6. Add the spices and stir-fry for a couple minutes, until fragrant.

7. Add the chopped tomatoes, stir and cook for 5 minutes.

8. When the mixture becomes mushy add the cauliflower and cashew nuts. Stir well together.

9. Add the water and coconut cream. Mix well.

10. Bring to boil. Cover the pot and cook over medium heat for about 12-15 minutes depending how tender you like your cauliflower.

11. Remove from the heat. Add salt and pepper to taste, fresh coriander and stir.

12. Cover and let it rest for 5 minutes before serving.

13.

50. Grilled Avocado Stuffed with Broccoli and Tofu

This might sound like a strange recipe, because when we think of avocado we usually think of guacamole and salads.

Don't be put off, though. The flavor and simplicity of this dish will surprise you.

Preparation time: 40 minutes

Cooking time: 10-15 minutes

Serves: 4

Ingredients:

- ¼ cup extra virgin olive oil
- 1 tbsp. grainy mustard
- 1 clove of garlic – chopped
- Pinch of chilli flakes
- ½ tsp. ground cumin
- ½ cup of fresh parsley – roughly chopped
- Juice of 1 lemon
- Zest of ½ lemon – grated
- Salt & Pepper to taste
- 1 pack of extra firm or firm tofu – cut into ½ inch cubes
- 2 stalks of broccoli – remove and discard stems, cut florets into medium pieces
- 3 ripe avocados – need to be firm

Preparation:

1. Put the olive oil, mustard, garlic, chilli flakes, lemon Juice, lemon zest, salt, pepper and cumin in a small bowl. Whisk all ingredients together to make a marinade mix then set aside.

2. Put the broccoli and tofu into a large dish and pour the marinade over.

3. Cover the dish and refrigerate for at least 30 minutes.

4. While the broccoli and tofu are marinading, preheat the grill to high.

5. Cut the avocado in halves and remove the pits

6. Brush the inside of the avocados with some olive oil and sprinkle with salt and pepper and set aside.

7. Place the broccoli and tofu in a grilling tray under the grill and grill until tender and with brown bits. Make sure you do not place them too close to the grill or they will burn.

8. When ready remove from the grill, add fresh parsley and gently toss.

9. Place the avocado halves under the grill until the start coloring.

10. Spoon the broccoli and tofu into the avocado halves, drizzle a little bit of olive oil on top and serve.

51. Eggplant and Coconut Milk Curry with Cauliflower "Rice"

Eggplant is an excellent low-carb vegetable with a unique texture and very distinguished flavor. It is very nutritious and a good source of dietary fiber.

It pairs very well with the cauliflower rice. You can use the cauliflower rice raw, or you can cook it in the microwave for 5 minutes (or steam it on the stove).

Preparation time:10 minutes

Cooking time: 25 minutes

Serves: 4

Ingredients:

- 1 lb. eggplant – skin on and cut into 1 inch pieces
- ½ white onion – diced
- 1 inch piece of ginger – minced
- 2 cloves of garlic – minced
- ½ cup Cashew nuts
- 3 tbsp. coconut oil
- 1 cup coconut milk
- 1 tbsp. mild curry powder
- Salt & Pepper to taste
- ½ cup fresh coriander – roughly chopped

For the Cauliflower "Rice":

- 1 large cauliflower – stem removed, florets cut into medium pieces

Preparation:

1. Start by making the cauliflower "rice".

2. Put the cauliflower florets in a food processor with a grating blade. A regular blade will also do.

3. Pulse until the cauliflower looks like rice. Make sure not to overdo or you will end up with a mash.

4. If you do not have a food processor, you can use a hand grater.

5. Set the rice aside.

6. Put the coconut oil in a large frying pan and heat over medium-high heat.

7. When the oil is hot, add the eggplant and cook for approximately 5 minutes until the eggplant is seared. Stir occasionally.

8. Add onion, garlic, ginger and cook until soft while stirring.

9. You can add a little bit more oil if necessary as the eggplant tends to absorb most of it.

10. Add curry powder and stir well.

11. After about 1 minute add cashew nuts, coconut milk, black pepper and a pinch of salt.

12. Simmer for about 5 minutes or until the sauce is slightly reduced.

13. Take off the heat and add fresh coriander. Stir gently and serve.

52. Pan-Seared Tempeh Steak with Roasted Cabbage and Walnuts

This recipe contains everything your body needs for the perfect low-carb, high-fat regime by combining the tempeh, cabbage, nuts and a good amount of extra virgin olive oil.

Preparation time: 1 hour

Cooking time: 40 minutes

Serves: 4

Ingredients:

For the Pan-Seared Tempeh:
- 1 lb. tempeh – cut into 3 ½ inch long by 3/8 inch thick slices
- ¼ cup water
- 1 garlic clove – minced
- 1 tsp. dried oregano
- ¼ tsp. pepper flakes
- ¾ cup extra virgin olive oil
- 6 tbsp. red wine vinegar

For the Roasted Cabbage:
- 1 medium head of green cabbage – cut into 8 wedges and core trimmed.
- Juice of 1 lemon
- 2 tbsp. extra virgin olive oil
- Salt & Pepper

Preparation:

1. Preheat oven to 450F.

2. In a plastic sealable bag combine the water, red wine vinegar, garlic, oregano and pepper flakes. Add tempeh, press out the air and seal the bag.

3. Toss the bag to completely coat the tempeh with the marinade.

4. If you do not have a sealable bag you can use a mixing ball and cover it with cling film.

5. Refrigerate your tempeh for 1 hour. You can marinade for longer if you have time.

6. Place wedges on a roasting tray. Arrange them in a single layer.

7. Sprinkle walnuts on top.

8. In a small bowl whisk together the extra virgin olive oil and lemon juice.

9. Pour the mixture on top of the cabbage and season with salt and pepper to taste.

10. Gently toss the wedges to completely coat with the mixture.

11. Roast each side of the cabbage for approximately 15 minutes until nicely browned.

12. After 1 hour, remove tempeh from the marinade.

13. Pat tempeh dry with a piece of paper towel.

14. Take a large skillet or frying pan and heat the olive oil over medium heat.

15. When the oil is hot add tempeh and cook for about 2-4 minutes until golden brown.

16. Turn tempeh on the other side and reduce heat. Cook for another 2-4 minutes.

17. Remove from the heat and move tempeh onto a sheet of paper towel over a plate.

18. Serve on a plate with the cabbage.

19. You can top with a drizzle of extra virgin olive oil.

53. Scrambled Tofu with Guacamole

If you do not have much time to cook dinner, but still want to benefit from healthy ingredients, this is a very easy and quick recipe to whip up a tasty main course in no time.

This is such a delish and light meal that can also be made for a savory breakfast.

Preparation time: 10 minutes

Cooking time: 10 minutes

Serves: 4

Ingredients:

- ½ white onion – diced
- 1 stick of celery – diced
- 1 courgette – diced
- 1 green capsicum - diced
- 2 cloves garlic - minced
- 1 inch piece of ginger – minced
- 1 lb. firm tofu
- ½ bunch fresh coriander – roughly chop leaves and finely chop stalks
- 2 tbsp. coconut oil
- 1 tbsp. ground turmeric
- 1 tbsp. ground cumin
- 3 tbsp. tamari sauce
- Ground Black Pepper
- ½ cup pumpkin seeds

For Guacamole:

- 2 large soft avocados
- Juice of 2 large limes or lemons
- Salt & Pepper
- 1 large tomato - diced

Preparation:

1. Drain tofu and pat dry with paper towel.

2. Crumble tofu.

3. Prepare the guacamole. Cut avocados in half and remove pits.

4. Scoop avocados into a bowl. Add lime juice, salt and pepper and mash.

5. Add the diced tomato and stir to combine. Set aside.

6. Heat the coconut oil in a deep frying pan over medium-low heat.

7. Add all the diced vegetables to the frying pan.

8. Stir continuously and cook until tender.

9. Add garlic, ginger and coriander stalks.

10. Stir and cook for another minute.

11. Add all the spices and stir to coat.

12. Add tofu and stir until tofu is evenly coated with spices.

13. Remove from the heat.

14. Stir in coriander and tamari sauce. Sprinkle with ground black pepper.

15. Serve topped with lots of avocado and garnish with pumpkin seeds.

54. Cauliflower Couscous with Roasted Vegetables

This super healthy dish benefits from the low carb content of cauliflower couscous instead of using the real couscous, which is much higher in carbs.

We have added almonds for extra crunchiness and nuttiness, and pared it with juicy veggies roasted in plenty of extra virgin olive oil.

Preparation time: 30 minutes

Cooking time: 35 minutes

Serves: 4

Ingredients:

For the Cauliflower Couscous:
- 1 medium cauliflower – cut into large florets – stems removed
- 1 cup fresh parsley – roughly chopped
- ½ cup roasted almonds – crushed

For the Roasted Vegetables:
- 2 eggplants – skin on and cut into 1 inch pieces
- 2 green capsicums – diced into 1 inch pieces
- 2 cups of button mushrooms – cut into halves
- 1 broccoli head – florets cut into halves
- 3 tbsp. olive oil

- 2 cloves garlic – crushed
- ½ cup fresh coriander – roughly chopped
- Salt & Pepper

Preparation:

1. Preheat oven to 392F.

2. Fill a saucepan with water and bring to boil.

3. When water boils drop cauliflowers in. Cook for 3 minutes.

4. Drain and cool under cold water. Drain well.

5. Place the florets into a food processor; add parsley and pulse to obtain a fine crumb.

6. Move the crumbs into a bowl and add roasted almonds. Combine together and set aside.

7. Place vegetables on a baking tray.

8. Add garlic, thyme, extra virgin olive oil, salt and pepper to taste and toss well together.

9. When oven is hot place in oven and roast for 30 minutes.

10. Remove from the oven and serve over the cauliflower couscous.

11. Top with a drizzle of extra virgin olive oil and fresh coriander.

55. Tempeh Curry Laksa Style with Kelp Noodles

This exotic recipe is inspired by the Laksa dishes, originally from Malaysia and Indonesia.

We used coconut milk for a creamy texture, kelp noodles for their low carb content, and tempeh for its delicious nutty flavor and high amount of protein.

Preparation time: 10-15 minutes

Cooking time: 30 minutes

Serves: 4

Ingredients:

- ½ lb. Tempeh – cut into 1 inch cubes
- Coconut oil
- 1 small chili – deseeded and finely sliced
- 2 cloves of garlic – minced
- 1 inch piece of ginger – minced
- 1/ white onion - finely chopped
- 1 medium eggplant – cut into 1 inch pieces
- ¼ cup Laksa paste
- 6 curry leaves
- 1 ½ cup vegetable stock
- 1 can coconut milk
- 2 x 11 oz. packs kelp noodles
- 2/3 cup fresh coriander – roughly chopped
- Salt & Pepper
- Juice of 1 lime

To Serve:

- 1/2 cup Cashew nuts
- ½ cup coriander – finely chopped
- 1 spring onion – finely sliced
- Lime wedges

Preparation:

1. Heat ¼ cup of coconut oil in a frying pan over medium-high heat.

2. Cook tempeh in 2 separate batches until golden brown.

3. Remove from the pan and set aside on a sheet of paper towel.

4. Place a big tablespoon of coconut oil in a saucepan and place over medium heat.

5. Add the onion, chili, garlic, ginger, curry leaves and Laksa paste.

6. Stir well and cook for 4 minutes.

7. Add the eggplant and a pinch of salt. Stir well until eggplant is coated with the spices and cook for another 4 minutes. If the pan is too dry, add an extra spoon of coconut oil.

8. Add vegetable stock, coconut milk and a sprinkle of ground black pepper.

9. Bring to boil and lover the heat to low.

10. Cover the pan and simmer for 15 minutes. Stir occasionally.

11. Remove the pot from the heat. Stir in the chopped coriander, fried tempeh and lime juice.

12. Remove kelp noodle from their package and rinse with cold water and cut them in half with a kitchen scissor.

13. Add the noodles to the curry pot and stir gently.

14. Divide the curry into bowls and top with fresh coriander, spring onions and cashew nuts.

15. Serve hot with extra lime wedges.

56. Walnut Stuffed Eggplant with Rocket Salad

We brought the eggplant back for another great recipe.

The walnuts will add a kind of "meaty" texture, plus lots of protein and healthy fats to this easy-to-make meal.

Preparation time: 15-20 minutes

Cooking time: 40 minutes

Serves: 2

Ingredients:

- 1 large long eggplant – cut in half lengthwise
- 1 cup walnuts
- 2 medium-large ripe tomatoes - chopped
- 2 cloves of garlic – chopped
- ½ red onion – diced
- 2 tbsp. extra virgin olive oil
- Salt & Pepper to taste
- ½ cup fresh parsley – roughly chopped

For the Salad:

- 7 oz. rocket leaves
- 1 cup cherry tomatoes – cut into halves
- 1 tbsp. extra virgin olive oil
- 1 tsp. balsamic vinegar
- Juice of ½ lemon
- Salt & Pepper

Preparation:

1. Preheat oven to 356F.

2. Place walnuts in a food processor and pulse until the texture resembles minced meat. Set Aside.

3. Place the eggplant on a baking tray and with a knife cut the centre flesh into diagonal crisscross.

4. Drizzle with extra virgin olive oil and sprinkle with salt and pepper.

5. When oven is hot, put the eggplant in the oven and bake for approximately 20 minutes.

6. Leave to cool for few minutes, then scoop out the flesh and place into a bowl.

7. Heat the oil in a frying pan over medium heat. Add garlic and red onion and sauté until soft and lightly tanned.

8. Add the tomatoes with a pinch of salt and pepper and cook for 2-3 minutes until soft. Stir occasionally. If the pan is too dry you can add a table spoon of water.

9. Stir in the eggplant and walnuts. Keep cooking for another 5 minutes.

10. Remove from heat, add fresh parsley and stir.

11. Stuff the eggplant with the mixture.

12. Put back in the oven and bake for about 10 minutes.

13. In a large salad bowl place the rocket and cherry tomatoes.

14. Add a pinch of salt and pepper. Pour the olive oil, balsamic vinegar and lemon juice. Toss gently.

15. Serve the stuffed eggplant while still hot with the rocket salad on the side.

57. Broccoli and Zucchini Patties with Avocado and Walnut Salad

Why not have a burger without a bun? This is a great substitute for a meat burger, and it will taste delicious together with a high-fat salad of avocado and nuts.

Preparation time: 20 minutes

Cooking time: 10-15 minutes

Serves: 4

Ingredients:
- 1 large head of broccoli – stem removed and cut into florets
- 2 cups raw zucchini – peeled and chopped
- 2 tbsp. ground flaxseeds
- 2 tsp. Tamari sauce
- 1 tbsp. Dijon mustard
- 2 cloves garlic – minced
- Salt & Pepper
- 2 tbsp. whole-wheat breadcrumbs
- Extra virgin olive oil

For the Avocado Salad:
- 4 hearts Romaine lettuce – chopped
- 2 medium soft avocados – diced
- 1 cup cherry tomatoes – cut into halves
- ½ cup walnuts
- 1 tsp. grainy mustard
- 2 tbsp. extra virgin olive oil

- Juice of ½ lemon
- 1 tsp. balsamic vinegar
- Salt & Pepper

Preparation:

1. Preheat oven to 400F.

2. Line a baking tray with baking paper and place broccoli florets on top.

3. Drizzle with extra virgin olive oil and add a sprinkle of salt and pepper.

4. Toss well until evenly coated.

5. Put in the oven and bake for 15 minutes.

6. Take out of oven and late broccoli cool down.

7. When broccoli have cooled down place in a food processor together with the flax seeds, zucchini, Dijon mustard, salt and pepper.

8. Processes until all ingredients are well combined.

9. Add breadcrumbs and stir well with a spoon. Make 4 firm patties.

10. Put 2 tablespoons of extra virgin olive oil in a large frying pan over medium heat.

11. Cook your patties for approximately 5-6 minutes per side, until golden brown.

12. Set the patties aside on a paper towel and keep warm.

13. In a large bowl combine the Romaine lettuce, avocado, cherry tomatoes and walnuts.

14. In a small bowl whisk together grainy mustard, lemon juice, salt and pepper, balsamic vinegar and olive oil. Whisk until obtaining a creamy vinaigrette. If your vinaigrette is too thick you can dilute with couple drops of water.

15. Pour the vinaigrette over salad and gently toss.

16. Serve the patties warm with avocado salad on the side.

58. Broccoli Bisque with a Twist

This soup is a true combination of flavors and goodness, perfect for a quick lunch or dinner.

Preparation time: 20 minutes (excluding soaking)

Cooking time: 15 minutes

Serves: 2

Ingredients:

- 8 oz. fresh broccoli
- 2 ½ cups of water
- 1 cup raw cashew nuts - soaked and drained
- 1/2 clove of garlic
- 1 small soft avocado
- Juice of 1 lime or lemon
- Salt & Pepper to taste
- 1 tbsp. olive oil (optional)

Preparation:

1. Put the raw cashew nuts into a bowl, cover and leave to soak 6-8 hours or overnight.

2. Pour the water into a saucepan and bring to the boil.

3. Wash and split broccoli removing the hard parts of the stems but keeping most of them.

4. Once the water is boiling, add the broccoli and lightly boil until tender.

5. Drain the broccoli and save the water for later.

6. Drain and rinse the cashews.

7. Combine the cashews, broccoli, avocado and the water to a blender and blend at high speed until smooth and creamy.

8. Pour the mixture into a saucepan and warm up on a low heat while stirring occasionally until bubbles start forming.

9. If the mixture is too thick you can add a little bit of water.

10. Take off the heat, add lemon juice and salt & pepper to taste. Stir and taste.

11. You can adjust salt & pepper if needed or add more lemon to taste.

12. Pour your bisque into two bowls and garnish with some cashews and a drizzle of olive oil.

59. Cream of Spinach Soup

This is another excellent soup that is high in protein and fat. It is very filling and nutritious, and can be served as a light meal.

Preparation time: 30 minutes

Cooking time: 30 minutes

Serves: 4-5

Ingredients:

- 1 tbsp. olive oil
- 2 cloves of garlic - chopped
- 3.5 oz. white onion - sliced
- 1 oz. celery - diced
- 5 oz. green beans - diced
- 0.4 oz. parsley - finely chopped
- 3 oz. spinach
- 4 cups vegetable broth
- 1.2 oz. raw almonds - soaked
- Salt & Pepper to taste

Preparation:

1. Put the raw almonds in a bowl, cover and soak overnight.

2. In a large saucepan heat the olive oil over a medium heat.

3. Add the onion and sauté for 5 minutes until translucent.

4. Add the garlic, celery, green beans, a pinch of salt and sauté for another 5 minutes.

5. Add the vegetable broth and stir. Turn the heat to high, cover the pot and bring to boil. When the soup starts boiling, reduce the heat to low and simmer for 10 minutes.

6. Add the spinach and simmer for an additional 10 minutes.

7. Remove the saucepan from the heat and leave it to cool.

8. Drain the almonds and add them to the soup.

9. When the soup has cooled down a little, pour it in batches into a blender and blend on high speed for approximately 40 seconds until smooth and creamy. Blend longer if necessary.

10. You can return the soup to the saucepan and warm up or you can eat it straight away. Both ways it will taste delicious.

11. Add some ground black and serve.

60. Green Cauliflower Soup

The trick with soup is to keep it simple. Something as basic as cauliflower can make a deliciously creamy and tasty low carb vegan-friendly soup.

The extra olive oil will add the good fats and a Mediterranean flavor perfect for a starter.

Preparation time: 25 minutes

Cooking time: 25 minutes

Serves: 8

Ingredients:

- 1 tbsp. extra virgin olive oil
- 1 medium white onion - chopped
- 3 cloves of garlic - chopped
- 3 lb. cauliflower (florets and stems) - cut into chunky pieces
- 5 cups of water
- 1/2 fresh parsley - roughly chopped
- 2 oz. green beans - chopped
- 1 oz. green beets - roughly chopped
- Salt & Pepper to taste
- Juice of 1/2 lemon

Preparation:

1. Heat the oil in a large saucepan over a medium heat.

2. Add onion and let it cook for approximately 5 minutes until translucent and soft.

3. Add garlic and stir. Add a pinch of salt and let it cook for a further 2-3 minute until garlic becomes golden or lightly tanned. Make sure not to burn the garlic.

4. Add cauliflower and stir. Pour in the water until it covers the cauliflower. Stir again.

5. Cover the pot and bring to boil over a high heat.

6. When the soup starts boiling, bring the heat to low and simmer gently for about 10 minutes or until the cauliflower is tender.

7. Add all your greens, stir and let simmer for another 3-5 minutes.

8. Take the soup off the heat, add the chopped parsley.

9. Let the soup cool for about 10 minutes.

10. Puree the soup with a blender until very smooth and creamy. If the soup is too thick for your taste you can add a little bit of water.

11. Return the soup to a low heat and warm up until bubbles form.

12. Take off the stove, add lemon juice, salt, and pepper to taste and stir.

13. Garnish with parsley and a drizzle of olive oil. Serve immediately.

61. Winter Italian Minestrone

Minestrone is the ultimate "cozy soup". It's tasty, filling and it provides your body with most of the minerals needed for a healthy diet.

It is deliciously hot on a cold winter day, or at room temperature on a warm summer day.

You can make a big batch and store it in the fridge for up to 5 days, or freeze it for few months.

Preparation time: 25 minutes

Cooking time: 45 minutes

Serves: 8

Ingredients:

- 2 tbsp. coconut oil
- 1/2 cup white onion - diced
- 2 cloves of garlic - chopped
- 3 carrots - chopped
- 1 cup of mushrooms - chopped
- 2 courgettes - chopped
- 3 oz. broccoli - florets halved and stems chopped
- 1/2 cup green beans - chopped
- 2 large tomatoes - chopped
- 3 oz. cabbage
- 5 cups of water
- 1 tbsp. olive oil
- Juice of 1 lemon
- 1/2 cup parsley
- Salt & pepper to taste

Preparation:

1. Wash and prep all your veggies.

2. In a large saucepan, heat the coconut oil on a medium heat.

3. Add onion, stir, and cook for approximately 5 minutes, until tender.

4. Stir in the garlic and cook for another 2 minutes.

5. Add carrots, mushrooms, cabbage, tomatoes, and a pinch of salt. Stir well so that the veggies get the flavour from the onion and garlic

6. Add water, stir gently and bring to boil.

7. Cover, lower the heat to low and let simmer for 25 minutes. Stir occasionally.

8. Add broccoli, zucchini, and green beans and cook for another 10 minutes.

9. Take off the heat. Add parsley, lemon juice, olive oil and freshly ground black pepper. If needed adjust salt to taste. Let your minestrone rest for 5 minutes before serving.

62. Indian-Style Green Pepper, Courgettes, and Spinach Soup

This is an exotic low-carb soup with a kick — thanks to the added Indian spices.

The coconut milk will also make sure it's deliciously creamy. Yum!

Preparation time: 20 minutes

Cooking time: 45 minutes

Serves: 4-5

Ingredients:

- 1 small white onion - chopped
- 2 cloves of garlic - chopped
- 2 tbsp. coconut oil
- 1 tbsp. mild curry powder
- 3 medium size green peppers - chopped in large pieces
- 3 large courgettes - chopped into 1/2-inch round pieces
- 8 oz. spinach - roughly chopped
- 1 large tomato - chopped
- 2 tsp. tomato paste
- 1 can coconut milk
- 1 cup of water
- Juice of 2 limes
- 1/2 cup of coriander
- Salt & Pepper to taste

Preparation:

1. Heath the coconut oil in a large saucepan on a medium heat.

2. Add the onion and cook approximately 5 minutes, until tender and translucent.

3. Add garlic, stir and cook for another 2-3 minutes until garlic takes on a nice tanned color.

4. Stir in the curry powder and cook for 2 minutes, until fragrant.

5. Add the chopped tomatoes and tomato paste and a pinch of salt. Mash all ingredients together and cook for another 5 minutes until you have a creamy paste.

6. Add coconut milk and water. Stir and bring to boil.

7. Cover the pot, lower the heat to low and simmer for 5 minutes.

8. Add green peppers and courgettes. Turn the heat up to medium-high and bring to boil again.

9. Turn the heat down to low and simmer for 25 minutes.

10. Take off the heat, add lime juice, coriander and freshly ground black pepper. Add salt to taste if necessary.

11. Let your soup rest for 5 minutes and serve.

Extras

63. Cucumber Bites

These fresh and tasty cucumbers bites can really be enjoyed at any time of the day. Cucumber is low carb and refreshing; you will not feel guilty for nibbling away at these wonderful treats.

Preparation time: 10 minutes (excluding soaking time)

Soaking time: 1-3 hours

Serves: 14 bites

Ingredients:
- 1 cup almonds – soaked 1-3 hours
- ¼ cup cashew nuts – soaked 1-3 hours
- Juice of 1 lemon
- 1 clove garlic –minced
- Salt & Pepper
- 1 tsp. olive oil
- 1 large cucumber – sliced into approximately 1 inch pieces
- 1 tomato – diced
- ½ cup fresh parsley – roughly chopped

Preparation:

1. Soak almonds and cashew nuts in warm water for 1-3 hours. The longer you soak them, the softer and creamier they will be.

2. Put all ingredients (except cucumber, parsley and tomato) into a blender or food processor.

3. Blend or process until you get a creamy paste.

4. If the mix is too thick for your likings you can add a little bit of water.

5. Remove the mixture from the blender.

6. Add the diced tomato and fresh parsley and gently mix with a spoon.

7. Scoop one spoonful of mixture onto each cucumber slice.

8. Sprinkle with black pepper and serve.

64. Broccoli Crispy Bread

This incredible vegan flatbread is enriched with protein from the chia seeds.

You can enjoy this bread as a snack, or as a compliment to your main meal.

Preparation time: 5 minutes

Cooking time: 30 minutes

Serves: 3-4

Ingredients:

- 4 cups of broccoli florets – cut into chunks
- 3 tbsp. nutritional yeast
- 1 tbsp. extra virgin olive oil
- 2 tbsp. chia seeds
- 1 tsp. baking powder
- Salt & Pepper
- ½ cup fresh basil

Preparation:

1. Preheat oven to 375F.

2. Soak the chia seeds with 6 tablespoons of water for about 5 minutes.

3. Put broccoli into a food processor and pulse until you get a texture similar to rice.

4. Add nutritional yeast, basil, salt and pepper, and pulse until ingredients are well combined.

5. Transfer the mix into a bowl, add olive oil, baking powder, chia seeds and stir well.

6. Line a baking tray with a sheet of baking paper.

7. Pour the dough onto the baking paper and spread evenly. The thinner you make it, the crispier it will be.

8. Bake in the oven for approximately 30 minute until golden and crispy. Make sure it is cooked in the middle.

9. Remove from the oven and cut into bars.

10. Enjoy while still warm or cold.

65. Roasted Pumpkin Seeds

Roasted pumpkin seeds are simply awesome to nibble on, or to add to your soups or salads.

They are a great source of magnesium and zinc, and one of the best sources of plant-based omega-3s.

Preparation time: 5 minutes

Cooking time: 25 minutes

Serves: As many as you'd like

Ingredients:
- Pumpkin Seeds
- Extra virgin olive oil
- Salt & Pepper

Preparation:
1. Preheat oven to 350F.

2. Line a baking tray with baking paper or aluminium foil. Either will do.

3. Place the seeds into a bowl, drizzle with not too much oil but enough to evenly coat them.

4. Sprinkle with salt and pepper and toss well together.

5. Pour the seeds onto the baking tray and roast in the oven for approximately 20 minutes or until they become very lightly brown. Keep an eye on them not to burn them.

6. During cooking remove the tray a few times to stir the seeds.

7. When completely roasted, remove from oven and let them cool.

8. Enjoy as nibbles or sprinkle on your salad or soup.

66. Multi Seeds Crackers

These super healthy crackers are perfect to enjoy plain, or with the dip of your choice.

They are delicious, crispy and full of good fats and protein provided by the different types of seeds.

Preparation time: 10 minutes

Cooking time: 1 hour

Serves: 20-30 crackers (depending on your cuts)

Ingredients:
- ½ cup chia seeds
- ½ cup sunflower seeds
- ½ cup pumpkin seeds
- ½ cup sesame seeds
- 1 cup water
- 1 large clove garlic or 2 small – minced
- Salt & Pepper

Preparation:
1. Preheat oven to 300F.

2. Put all seeds into a large bowl and add water. Stir well until combined.

3. Let the seeds rest for 3-5 minutes until the chia seeds absorb the water.

4. Stir again. There should be no more water on the bottom of the bowl.

5. Use a spatula to spread the mixture onto the baking paper. Spread into two rectangles approximately 12"x 7" in size and approximately 1/8 to ¼ inch thick.

6. Sprinkle with salt and pepper.

7. Bake in the oven for 35 minutes.

8. Remove from oven and turn the rectangles around very carefully with a spatula.

9. Put back in the oven and back for another 25-35 minutes.

10. Keep an eye on them to make sure they don't burn.

11. Remove from oven when the edges are lightly golden.

12. Set aside to cool down for approximately 10 minutes.

13. Break the rectangles into crackers and let to cool completely.

14. You can store these crackers in an airtight container for up to 1 month, but we honestly think they will not last you that long as they are too moreish!

67. Almond Cauliflower

This one is perfect to taste as a nibble and appetizer. It can also be a great choice of side to one of your main dishes.

Preparation time: 5 minutes

Cooking time: 30 minutes

Serves: 4

Ingredients:

- 4 cups cauliflower florets – chopped into bite size chunks
- 1 tbsp. extra virgin olive oil
- 2 tbsp. almonds – chopped in very small pieces

Preparation:

1. Preheat oven to 425F.

2. Line a baking tray with baking paper.

3. Place cauliflower into a bowl, add olive oil, salt and pepper, almonds and toss everything well together.

4. Pour the cauliflower onto the baking paper.

5. Bake in oven for approximately 30 minutes or until golden brown and soft. Stir occasionally.

6. Remove from oven, sprinkle with ground black pepper and serve.

68. Tahini Dressing

This dressing is not only delicious and versatile, but it is also full of healthy properties thanks to the tahini paste.

Tahini is made out of sesame seeds, which are an excellent source of copper, omega-3 and omega-6.

Preparation time: 5 minutes

Serves: 4-5

Ingredients:
- ¼ cup tahini paste
- Juice of 1 lemon
- 1 tbsp. apple cider vinegar
- 2 tbsp. extra virgin olive oil
- 2 cloves of garlic – minced
- Salt & Pepper

Preparation:
1. Placc all ingredients into a blender (except for water).

2. Blend until creamy.

3. If the dressing is too thick, add a little bit of water until it reaches the desired consistency.

69. Lemon & Mustard Vinaigrette

This is an all-time favorite, it goes well on any salad, and it is both keto and vegan friendly.

Preparation time: 5 minutes

Serves: 6 tablespoons

Ingredients:
- Juice of 1 lemon
- ½ tsp. Dijon mustard
- 4 tbsp. extra virgin olive oil
- Salt & Pepper

Preparation:
1. Put lemon juice, mustard, salt and pepper into a bowl.

2. Whisk well until combined.

3. While whisking, drizzle in the extra virgin olive oil.

4. Keep whisking vigorously until all ingredients are combined and you have a medium creamy dressing.

5. The dressing should be ready at this point. You can taste and adjust any of the ingredients to taste.

70. Cheesy Sauce

This "veganized" cheesy sauce is rich in both taste and texture. It works great as a topping for roasted veggies or vegan burger patties.

Preparation time: 5 minutes

Serves: 4

Ingredients:

- 2 tbsp. extra virgin olive oil
- 2 tbsp. nutritional yeast
- Juice of 1 lemon
- Salt & Pepper

Preparation:

1. Combine all ingredients together into a bowl and whisk vigorously.

2. Serve as an accompaniment to your dishes.

71. Chimichurri Style Sauce

This sauce is a combination of great flavors and herbs, very similar to the Argentinian Chimichurri.

You can drizzle this on top of your veggies, salads and soups — you can even use it as a dip!

Preparation time: 1-2 minutes

Cooking time: 5 minutes

Serves: 2/3 cup

Ingredients:

- ½ cup extra virgin olive oil
- 1 tsp. fresh rosemary
- 1 tsp. fresh oregano
- 2 medium cloves garlic – crushed
- 2 tsp. smoked paprika
- 1 bay leaf
- ¼ tsp. sea salt
- 1 tbsp. lemon juice
- Pinch of black pepper flakes

Preparation:

1. Put the herbs into a mortar and pestle and lightly pound them. If you do not have a mortar and pestle you can chop them very finely.

2. Pour olive oil into a pan and warm over medium-low heat.

3. When oil is hot, remove from heat.

4. Stir paprika, black pepper flakes, bay leaf and a pinch of salt into the oil.

5. Add herbs and lemon juice.

6. Put the sauce into a jar in the fridge and leave it to infuse for a couple of days before using.

72. Peanut Sauce

This very popular Asian sauce will be a winner with your Asian and non-Asian dishes alike. You can easily pair it with veggie skewers, for example.

Preparation time: 10 minutes

Cooking time: 5 minutes

Serves: 1 cup

Ingredients:
- ½ cup creamy peanut butter
- 2 tbsp. Thai red curry paste
- ¾ cup coconut milk
- 2tbsp. apple cider vinegar
- 1/2 tbsp. coconut palm sugar
- 2 tbsp. ground peanuts
- Salt

Preparation:
1. Add all ingredients together into a saucepan and whisk well.

2. Transfer the pan to the stove and heat up the mix over a low heat while continuing whisking.

3. Keep a constant eye on the sauce and as soon as it starts bubbling remove from heat. If you like the sauce more liquid, add a little bit of water and whisk.

4. Move the sauce into a bowl and top with ground peanuts.

73. Spicy Almond & Garlic Dip

This hummus-like creamy dip is delicious with raw vegetables or crackers.

It is very easy and quick to make, and you can keep it in the refrigerator for 3-4 days.

Preparation time: 5 minutes

Soaking time: Overnight

Serves: 1 large cup

Ingredients:

- 1 cup raw almonds
- 1 cup almond milk
- 2 cloves garlic
- ½ tsp. chili powder
- ¼ tsp. smoked paprika
- Pinch of salt
- Pinch of Cayenne pepper

Preparation:

1. Soak almonds overnight.

2. Put all ingredients into a blender.

3. Blend until smooth and creamy.

4. You can use immediately or refrigerate covered.

74. Cauliflower Hummus

You do not have to give up hummus to stick to your keto diet.

Try this great recipe that substitutes chick peas with low carb cauliflower.

Preparation time: 5 minutes

Cooking time: 5 minutes

Serves: 2 cups

Ingredients:

- 4 cups cauliflower stems and florets – chopped
- 2 tbsp. tahini paste
- 5 tbsp. extra virgin olive oil
- Juice of 2 lemons
- Salt & Pepper
- Pinch of cumin

Preparation:

1. Steam or lightly boil cauliflower for approximately 5 minutes or until soft.

2. Drain and let it cool down completely.

3. Combine cauliflower, tahini paste, extra virgin olive oil, lemon juice and cumin into a food processor. Process until creamy. Alternatively, you can use a blender.

4. Add salt and pepper to taste.

5. You might want to taste it and add more lemon juice or olive oil according to taste.

6. Serve with raw vegetables.

75. Eggplant & Walnut Spread

Eggplant together with walnuts is a winning combination. If you mix these two, you'll enjoy a delicious ketogenic vegan appetizer that you can use as a spread or dip, according to your likings.

Preparation time: 10-15 minutes

Cooking time: 45 minutes

Serves: 1 large cup

Ingredients:

- 2 x medium round eggplants
- 1 tbsp. extra virgin olive oil
- 1 cup walnuts – chopped
- 2 cloves garlic
- Juice of 1 large lemon
- Salt & Pepper
- 1 tsp. cumin
- 1/3 cup Tahini paste
- ½ cup fresh parsley leaves

Preparation:

1. Preheat oven to 375F.

2. Place eggplants on a baking tray and rub them with the olive oil.

3. Stab them with a knife a couple times.

4. Roast for 45 minutes until they look deflated and wrinkled.

5. In the meantime, toast the walnuts in a pan over medium-high heat for 3-4 minutes. Leave to cool

6. When eggplant is cooked, remove from oven and let it cool down.

7. Cut the eggplants in half and scoop the flesh out into a food processor.

8. Add walnuts and all other ingredients. Process until obtaining a paste.

9. Serve into a bowl with a drizzle of extra virgin olive oil accompanied by crackers or raw vegetables.

76. Coconut Yogurt Dip

You'll find a mix of creamy goodness in this coconut yogurt dip, enriched with garlic, cucumber and tangy lemon juice.

Preparation time: 10 minutes

Serves: 2 cups

Ingredients:

- 1 ½ cup coconut yogurt
- 1 large cucumber – peeled and cut into chunks
- 3 cloves garlic
- Juice of 1 lemon
- 2 tbsp. extra virgin olive oil
- ½ cup fresh coriander – finely chopped
- Salt & Pepper

Preparation:

1. Place all ingredients (except coriander) into a blender and blend until smooth.

2. Add salt and pepper to taste and the coriander.

3. Mix well with a spoon.

4. Refrigerate for about 1 hour to let the flavors infuse.

5. Stir the dip well before serving.

77. Olive Tapenade

A classic spread with all the goodness of olives. All it takes is 5 minutes.

Preparation time: 5 minutes

Serves: 1 cup

Ingredients:

- ½ cup black olives
- ½ cup green olives
- 2 cloves garlic
- 1tsp. lemon juice
- Ground black pepper

Preparation:

1. Put all ingredients together into a food processor and process for few seconds. You basically want all ingredients finely chopped and well mixed together. Be careful not processes for too long otherwise you will have a paste.

2. Serve to spread onto your favorite crackers.

78. Chunky Rocket Spread

This super healthy tangy spread can be shared as an appetizer with crackers, or you could use it to make canapes for a special dinner.

Preparation time: 15 minutes

Serves: 1 cup

Ingredients:

- 1 ½ cup roasted Cashew nuts
- 1 clove garlic
- 3 cups rocket leaves
- ¼ cup nutritional yeast
- ¼ cup extra virgin olive oil
- Juice of ½ lemon
- Salt & Pepper

Preparation:

1. Place the Cashew nuts, garlic and nutritional yeast into a food processor.

2. Pulse gently until the nuts are still chunky and mixed well together with the other ingredients. Then, transfer the mix into a bowl.

3. Place olive oil and lemon juice into the food processor, then add rocket leaves and pulse to blend.

4. Transfer the rocket mixture into the bowl with the Cashews, season with salt and pepper and mix together with a spoon. Serve with crackers or other low carb breads.

Snacks

79. Avocado Slices

For obvious reasons, fries are not a keto-friendly food.

Instead, try out these avocado slices, best served with creamy chili dip.

Preparation time: 5 minutes

Cooking time: 1 minutes

Serves: 2

Ingredients:

- 2 ripe avocados
- ¼ cup whipped coconut cream
- 1 cup almond meal
- 1 cup olive oil
- 1 pinch cayenne pepper
- Salt, to taste

Chili dip:

- 1 cup extra-virgin olive oil
- ½ cup almond milk
- 2 teaspoons cider vinegar
- 1 teaspoon chili powder
- Salt, to taste

Directions:

1. Peel, pit, and slice avocados.

2. Place whipped coconut cream in a small bowl.

3. In a separate bowl, combine almond meal with salt and cayenne pepper.

4. Heat oil in a deep pan.

5. Place avocado pieces into heated oil and fry 45 seconds.

6. Transfer to a paper lined plate.

7. Make a chili dip; blend all dip ingredients, except the oil in a food blender until smooth. Stream in oil and blend until creamy. Serve with avocado slices.

80. Kale Chips With Dip

Tasty kale chips – not soggy or burned, but perfectly seasoned and baked kale chips.

They are crunchy, highly addictive and great for the entire family.

Preparation time: 10 minutes

Cooking time: 12 minutes

Serves: 4

Ingredients:

- 1 bunch kale, torn into medium-sized pieces
- 2 tablespoons olive oil
- Salt, to taste
- Dried herbs or spices (basil, cayenne, chili) - optional

Dip:

- ½ cup avocado oil
- ¼ cup soy milk
- 1 clove garlic
- 2 tablespoons chopped parsley
- 1 teaspoon cider vinegar
- ¼ teaspoon chili powder
- Salt and white pepper, to taste

Directions:

1. Wash the kale, separate the leaves and stem and place onto kitchen towels to drain.

2. Torn kale into medium-sized pieces and place in a zip-lock bag with olive oil, salt, and desired seasoning.

3. Shake until each kale leaf is coated.

4. Heat oven to 350F and line two baking sheets with parchment paper.

5. Arrange the kale leaves onto baking sheets and bake 12 minutes.

6. In the meantime, make the dip; place ingredients in a jar or jug. Blend using an immersion blender until emulsified and smooth.

7. Serve kale chips with freshly prepared dip.

81. Almond Butter With Celery Sticks

Healthy snacks don't have to be difficult to make, and this recipe is a proof of it.

Preparation time: 25 minutes

Cooking time: 25 minutes

Serves: 4

Ingredients:
- 1 cup almonds
- ½ lb. celery sticks
- 1 pinch sea salt

Directions:
1. Heat oven to 250F and spread almonds onto a baking sheet.

2. Bake the almonds 25 minutes, stirring halfway through baking.

3. Transfer the almonds to a food processor. Add sea salt.

4. Process the almonds until smooth and creamy, stopping as needed to scrape down the blender sides. It takes around 25 minutes.

5. In the meantime, trim the celery and remove leaves.

6. Serve almond butter with celery.

82. Palm Fingers

Palm hearts have a very mild flavor. As they are very easy to prepare, they are the perfect option when you need some quick snacks.

Preparation time: 5 minutes

Cooking time: 5 minutes

Serves: 4

Ingredients:

- 2 14oz. can palm hearts, rinsed, cut into quarters
- 2 cups almond flour
- 1 cup whipped coconut cream
- 1 teaspoon Italian seasoning
- 1 teaspoon chili powder
- Salt, to taste
- Coconut oil, for frying

Dip:

- ½ cup raw hemp seeds
- ¼ cup avocado oil
- 4 tablespoons cashew milk
- 2 teaspoons fresh dill
- ¼ teaspoon dried garlic flakes
- 4 tablespoons water
- Salt and pepper, to taste

Directions:

1. Make the palm fingers; let the oil heat in a skillet.

2. In a small bowl, combine whipped coconut cream, and chili powder.

3. In a separate bowl, combine almond flour, Italian seasoning, some salt, and pepper.

4. Dip palm fingers into coconut cream and dredge through almond flour. Fry the palm hearts in heated oil for 2-3 minutes or until golden-brown.

5. Make the sauce; in a food blender, combine all ingredients, except the oil. Blend until smooth. While the blender is running low, stream in avocado oil. Blend until emulsified.

6. Serve palm fingers with prepared dip.

83. Avocado Mushroom Bombs

An irresistible, creamy, protein-rich and easy-to-make ketogenic, vegan snack.

Preparation time: 10 minutes + inactive time

Serves: 6

Ingredients:

- ½ large avocado
- ¼ cup coconut oil (not melted)
- 1 clove garlic, minced
- 1 chili pepper, seeded, chopped
- 2 tablespoons fresh chopped cilantro
- ½ tablespoon lime juice
- 1 cup sliced mushrooms
- 1 teaspoon olive oil
- Salt, to taste

Directions:

1. Heat olive oil in a skillet. Add mushrooms and cook for 6-8 minutes or until tender. Place it aside.

2. In a bowl, mash the avocado with coconut oil, garlic, chili pepper, cilantro, lime juice, and some salt.

3. Stir in the mushrooms and cover with a clean foil. Refrigerate 30 minutes.

4. Shape the mixture into 6 balls with an ice-cream scoop. Serve.

(Note: You can also roll the balls through almond meal.)

84. Ketogenic Tofu Bites

Tofu bites are rich in fiber, protein, and charged with an arsenal of health benefits.

Tofu has a bland taste, but with simple ingredients you can turn it into an outstanding snack.

Preparation time: 5 minutes

Cooking time: 5 minutes

Serves: 4

Ingredients:

- 1 package extra-firm tofu, drained
- 2 tablespoons sliced almonds
- 1 tablespoon white sesame seeds
- 1 tablespoon coconut oil
- 1 teaspoon walnut oil
- ¼ teaspoon dried garlic flakes
- 2 tablespoons coconut aminos
- ½ teaspoon red chili flakes
- 2 tablespoons filtered water
- Salt and pepper, to taste

Directions:

1. Cut tofu into 1-inch cubes.

2. Heat coconut oil in a skillet. Add tofu and cook for 2 minutes per side.

3. Add almonds and cook for 1 minute.

4. Add all the remaining ingredients and cook until sauce is reduced.

5. Serve with desired veggies.

85. Zucchini Rolls With Nut Butter

Healthy, easy to make, and done in no time. A great option if you're looking for a nutty fix.

Preparation time: 10 minutes

Cooking time: 2 minutes

Serves: 4

Ingredients:

- 3 medium zucchinis, trimmed
- 2 tablespoons olive oil
- Salt and pepper, to taste

Nut butter:

- 1 cup Brazil nuts
- 1 good pinch salt

Extras:

- 1 cup steamed and chopped broccoli

Directions:

1. Heat grill pan over medium-high heat.

2. Slice the zucchinis by a length to ¼-inch thick.

3. Brush the zucchini slices with olive oil on both sides and season with salt to taste.

4. Grill the zucchini slices for 4 minutes per side.

5. In the meantime, make nut butter. Toast Brazil nuts 2-3 minutes in a dry skillet over medium heat.

6. Leave the nuts to cool. Once cooled transfer into a food processor with a pinch of salt.

7. Process until you have a creamy and smooth mixture.

8. Spread nut butter over zucchini slices. Top with some broccoli and roll gently.

9. Serve immediately.

86. Fried Guacamole

These little guacamole balls are a very unique and tasty snack. You can serve them with a favorite dip or some fresh salad.

Preparation time: 10 minutes + inactive time

Cooking time: 5 minutes

Serves: 4

Ingredients:

- 2 ripe avocados
- 1 Jalapeno pepper, seeded, chopped
- ¼ cup almond meal
- 1 teaspoon chili powder
- 1 tablespoon fresh lime juice
- ½ teaspoon ground cumin
- Salt, to taste
- Coconut oil, for frying

Coating:

- ¼ cup ground flax seeds
- 2 tablespoons almond flour
- ½ teaspoon ground mustard seeds

Directions:

1. In a bowl, mash avocados. Add remaining ingredients and stir to combine.

2. Shape the mixture into walnut size balls and place in a freezer for 10 minutes just to harden.

3. In a wide plate combine flax seeds, almond flour, and ground mustard seeds.

4. Heat 2-inches coconut oil in a skillet.

5. Dredge guacamole balls through the almond mixture and drop carefully into heated oil.

6. Fry for 2-3 minutes or until golden.

7. Serve while still hot.

87. Green Smoothie

This smoothie is made with fresh ingredients, and are packed with vitamins, minerals, proteins, and even healthy fats.

We are sure you will love this emerald green, ketogenic-vegan smoothie.

Preparation time: 2 minutes

Serves: 1

Ingredients:

- 1 cup almond milk
- 1 ½ cups spinach
- 2 tablespoons MTC oil
- 4-6 ice cubes
- Few drops Stevia, to taste
- 1 large cucumber, peeled

Directions:

1. Combine all ingredients in a food blender.

2. Blend until smooth.

3. Serve immediately.

88. Icy Pops

Avocado Popsicles made with coconut milk, almond butter, and a hint of vanilla. They are creamy, rich, and everything you need from a frozen treat.

Preparation time: 5 minutes + inactive time

Serves: 4

Ingredients:
- 1 avocado, pitted, peeled
- 1 ½ teaspoons vanilla paste
- 1 cup coconut milk
- 2 tablespoons almond butter
- Few drops stevia, to taste
- ¼ teaspoon Ceylon cinnamon

Directions:
1. Combine all ingredients in a food blender.

2. Blend until smooth.

3. Transfer the mixture into popsicle molds and insert popsicle sticks.

4. Freeze 4 hours or until firm.

5. Serve.

89. Avocado & Raspberry Smoothie

Raspberries have many health benefits, including helping with weight loss and boosting the immune system.

You combine it with the fatty acids, vitamins and minerals of avocado, and you'll have a winning drink.

Preparation time: 2 minutes

Serves: 2

Ingredients:

- 1 ripe avocado – cut in half, pit and skin removed
- 1 cup water
- 1/3 cup coconut milk
- ½ cup fresh raspberries (you can use frozen if fresh are not available)
- 2 ice cubes (optional)

Preparation:

1. Add all ingredients into a blender.

2. Blend until smooth and creamy.

3. Serve in a glass.

90. Strawberry Coconut Smoothie

This must be the ultimate vegan keto smoothie. Incredibly quick to make!

We've included high-fat ingredients, such as coconut milk and almond butter, to give your low-carb strawberry drink some nice thickness.

Preparation time: 2 minutes

Serves: 2

Ingredients:
- 1 cup fresh strawberries
- 1 cup unsweetened coconut milk
- 2 tbsp. almond butter
- 2 ice cubes (optional)

Preparation:
1. Pour all ingredients into a blender.

2. Blend until smooth and creamy.

3. Serve in your favorite glass.

91. Thai Style Coconut Shake

This is a fitting shake for those sizzling summer days.

Close your eyes while drinking it, and you could see yourself relaxing on a tropical beach. Savor the goodness of coconut!

Preparation time: 2 minutes

Serves: 2

Ingredients:
- 2 cans full fat coconut milk
- Ice cubes

Preparation:
1. Pour coconut milk and 5-6 into a blender

2. Blend until ice is crushed.

3. Check thickness of your shake. The more ice you add, the thicker your shake will be.

4. Keep adding ice until you reach desired thickness.

5. Serve immediately into a tall glass garnished with an orchid flower (optional).

92. Frozen Berry Shake

This is another summer-day shake, perfect when you feel like having an ice cream.

You can choose any type of low-carb berries, depending on what's available.

Preparation time: 2 minutes

Serves: 2

Ingredients:

- 1 cup coconut cream
- 1 cup almond milk
- 1 cup mixed fresh berries (strawberries, raspberries, blueberries, depending what is available) – you can substitute with frozen berries if fresh ones are not accessible
- 2 cups ice

Preparation:

- Place all the ingredients into a blender.

- Blend until smooth and frozen.

- Serve immediately.

Desserts

93. Almond butter balls

Tasty bites with carob powder and rich almond butter.

If you do not like carob, you can use raw cocoa powder instead.

Preparation time: 10 minutes + inactive time

Serves: 14 balls

Ingredients:
- 3 tablespoons almond butter
- 3 tablespoons carob powder
- 3 teaspoons almond flour
- 2 teaspoons powdered Erythritol or Yacon powder
- ½ cup unsweetened coconut flakes

Directions:

1. In a bowl, combine almond butter, carob powder, almond flour, and Erythritol. Stir until combined.

2. Stir until combined.

3. Place coconut flakes in a small bowl.

4. Scoop prepared a mixture with a small ice cream scoop and drop into coconut flakes.

5. Roll until completely covered with the coconut flakes. Arrange the balls on a plate and refrigerate for 4-6 hour or until firm.

6. Serve and enjoy.

94. Cocoa Pumpkin Fudge

Creamy, smooth, melt-in-your-mouth fudge is a healthy dessert you can freely consume without feeling any guilt.

Preparation time: 10 minutes + inactive time

Serves: 24 slices

Ingredients:
- 1 cup organic unsweetened pumpkin puree
- 1 ¾ cups cocoa butter
- 1 teaspoon allspice
- 1 tablespoon melted coconut oil

Directions:
1. Line 8-inch glass dish with baking paper.

2. Melt cocoa butter over medium heat.

3. Stir in pumpkin puree and allspice. Stir to combine.

4. Add coconut oil and stir well. Transfer the mixture into a prepared glass dish and press down to distribute evenly.

5. Cover with a second piece of baking paper and refrigerate 2 hours.

6. Slice and serve.

95. Coconut Vanilla Panna Cotta

A quick dessert you can always make in no time, with only few ingredients. You will love its flavor and smooth texture.

Preparation time: 5 minutes + inactive time

Cooking time: 5 minutes

Serves: 6

Ingredients:

- 14oz. can full-fat coconut milk
- 1 tablespoon melted coconut oil
- 1 scoop vanilla flavored hemp seed protein powder
- 1 ½ teaspoons agar-agar powder
- ¼ cup shredded toasted coconut

Directions:

1. In a food blender, blend coconut milk, coconut oil, and protein powder.

2. Pour the mixture into the saucepan and stir in agar-agar powder.

3. Bring the mixture to a gentle simmer. Cook until agar-agar is completely dissolved and the mixture is thickened.

4. Grease 6 ramekins with coconut oil and pour in panna cotta.

5. Chill in the fridge for 2 hours.

6. Serve, garnished with toasted coconut.

96. Creamy Vanilla Custard

Light, creamy, and vanilla-flavored custard, made with macadamia nut butter.

Preparation time: 5 minutes

Cooking time: 5 minutes

Serves: 4

Ingredients:

- 1 cup full-fat coconut milk
- ½ cup coconut cream
- 1/3 cup macadamia nut butter
- 1/3 cup Yacon powder
- 1 teaspoon vanilla paste
- 1 teaspoon agar-agar powder

Directions:

1. Heat coconut milk in a saucepan.

2. Stir in macadamia nut butter, Yacon powder, and agar-agar.

3. Simmer gently until starts to thicken.

4. Stir in coconut cream and vanilla paste.

5. Divide mixture between four ramekins.

6. Chill in a fridge until set. Serve and enjoy.

97. Nutty Brownies

A no-fuss recipe, suitable for ketogenic-vegan diet followers, made with raw cocoa powder and macadamia nuts.

Preparation time: 10 minutes

Cooking time: 25 minutes

Serves: 9

Ingredients:

- ¾ cup macadamia nuts
- ¾ cup almond flour
- ¾ cup Yacon powder
- ¼ cup coconut oil
- 4 tablespoons cocoa butter
- 1 scoop chocolate flavored hemp seed protein powder
- 1 teaspoon vanilla extract
- 3 tablespoons raw cocoa powder
- 2 tablespoons flax seeds + ¼ cup water

Directions:

1. Heat oven to 350F and line 8-inch baking dish with a parchment paper.

2. In a small bowl, combine flax seeds with water. Place aside 10 minutes.

3. In a bowl, cream together Yacon powder, coconut oil, and cocoa butter.

4. Fold in the flax mixture and vanilla.

5. Add remaining ingredients, except the macadamia nuts.

6. Once you have a creamy batter, fold in the macadamia nuts.

7. Spread the batter into prepared baking dish and bake 25 minutes.

8. Remove the brownies from the oven and place aside to cool.

9. Slice before serving.

98. Refreshing "Fat Bombs"

Some may think the word "fat bomb" sounds negative, but this recipe is actually delicious and healthy — not all fat is bad!

With only a few ingredients, you can enjoy these refreshing lime-coconut fat bombs for a pleasant dessert.

Preparation time: 10 minutes + chill time

Serves: 8

Ingredients:

- 1 ½ teaspoons lime zest
- 1 tablespoon lime juice
- ¼ cup cocoa butter
- ¼ cup melted coconut oil
- Few drops stevia, to taste

Directions:

1. Prepare 8 silicone muffin cups.

2. Melt cocoa butter and coconut oil over a double boiler.

3. Sri in lime zest and lime juice, along with the desired amount of stevia.

4. Pour into silicone molds and place in the fridge.

5. Chill until hardened.

6. Remove from the molds and serve.

99. Chocolate Hemp Mousse

Raw cocoa powder and coffee are the main stars of this creamy and rich dessert.

If you need something airy, smooth, and elegant to treat your friends to, or to simply pamper yourself, then prepare this amazing mousse.

Preparation time: 10 minutes + inactive time

Serves: 4

Ingredients:

- 2 cups coconut cream
- 2 scoops cocoa flavored hemp protein powder
- ¼ cup chia seeds
- 7 drops stevia
- 1 teaspoon instant coffee
- Raw cocoa nibs, to sprinkle (optional)

Directions:

1. Place all ingredients in a large mixing bowl.

2. Whisk the ingredients until smooth.

3. Divide mixture between 4 dessert glasses.

4. Chill in a fridge for 3 hours.

5. Serve sprinkled with cocoa nibs.

100. Peanut Butter Cookies

These keto-friendly cookies have an enjoyable, smooth peanut butter flavor, with an added protein boost from the hemp powder.

Preparation time: 10 minutes

Cooking time: 10 minutes

Serves: 12

Ingredients:
- 1 cup smooth peanut butter
- ¾ cup almond flour
- ½ cup powdered Erythritol
- ¼ cup almond milk
- 1 scoop vanilla flavored hemp protein powder
- 1 teaspoon baking soda

Directions:
1. Heat oven to 350F and line a baking sheet with baking paper.

2. In a bowl, cream peanut butter, and powdered Erythritol.

3. In a separate bowl, combine all dry ingredients.

4. Fold the dry ingredients into peanut butter and stir until you have a crumbly mix.

5. Stir in almond milk and roll dough into balls (2 tablespoons per cookie).

6. Drop dough onto baking sheet and flatten with a fork, making a crisscross pattern.

7. Bake cookies 10 minutes. Cool completely before serving.

101. Comfort Cups

A neat-looking meal is always appreciated, but sometimes we just have to get a bit messy.

Anyway, who cares about neatness when you have a heavenly peanut butter-cacao dessert in front of you?

No one, and neither will you, once you try this simple yet delicious dessert.

Preparation time: 5 minutes + inactive time

Serves: 4

Ingredients:

- ¼ cup peanut butter
- 4 tablespoons coconut cream
- 4 tablespoons melted coconut oil
- 2 teaspoons cacao paste
- 8 drops Stevia

Directions:

1. Divide peanut butter between four silicone cups.

2. Divide remaining ingredients between the cups and stir to combine. Scrape down the cup sides.

3. Place in freezer 2 hours.

4. Remove from cups and serve.

102. Sweet Fritters With Lime

Almond-flour based fritters with a refreshing lime icing. Simple, smooth, satisfying.

Preparation time: 5 minutes

Cooking time: 5 minutes

Serves: 9

Ingredients:
- ½ cup almond flour
- 3 tablespoons powdered Erythritol
- 1 teaspoon baking soda
- ½ teaspoon guar gum
- 1 tablespoons flax seeds + 3 tablespoons water
- ½ tablespoon finely grated lime peel
- ½ teaspoon vanilla paste
- 2 cup coconut oil, for frying

Icing:
- 3 tablespoons powdered Erythritol
- 1 tablespoon fresh lime juice

Directions:

1. In a small bowl, combine flax and water. Place aside for 15 minutes.

2. In a medium-sized bowl, whisk almond flour, Erythritol, baking soda, guar gum, and lime peel.

3. Stir in flax mixture and vanilla paste.

4. Heat coconut oil in a small saucepan.

5. Drop batter by tablespoon into heated oil. Fry 2 minutes per side.

6. Repeat with remaining batter.

7. In the meantime, combine powdered Erythritol and lime juice until a smooth icing has formed.

8. Dip fritters into icing and arrange onto a plate.

9. Serve warm.

103. Quick Almond Butter Mousse

There is nothing more luscious than a creamy, velvety mousse. If you are a mousse lover, you cannot miss out on this quick-to-make, low-carb, high-fat mousse.

It works as the perfect ending to a healthy meal, or simply as a special treat anytime during the day. This mousse can also be frozen for an ice cream-like texture.

Preparation time: 10 minutes

Serves: 4

Ingredients:

- 2 x 13.5 oz. can full fat coconut milk – refrigerated overnight
- 4 tbsp. almond butter
- ½ tsp. liquid stevia
- ¼ cup almonds – chopped

Preparation:

1. Scoop the coconut cream at the top of the refrigerated cans of coconut milk into a bowl.

2. Add almond butter and stevia and whisk well. You can either use a manual or electric whisker.

3. Whisk until ingredients are well combined and you have a creamy fluffy mixture.

4. Pour the mousse into 4 small bowls.

5. You can serve immediately or put in the refrigerator to chill for approximately 1 hour. Alternatively, you can freeze for approximately 30 minutes.

6. Top with chopped almonds before serving.

104. Almond & Cocoa Mini Muffins

These mini muffins are keto-friendly since no flour is used.

Furthermore, the regular sugar is replaced by coconut palm sugar.

Enjoy them with a clean conscience!

Preparation time: 10 minutes

Cooking time: 18 minutes

Serves: 9 brownies

Ingredients:

- ¼ cup coconut palm sugar
- 3 tbsp. water
- 1 vanilla pod
- 1 tbsp. almond oil (it can be substituted with another nut oil or olive oil)
- 1 cup almonds
- ¼ cup hemp seeds
- 2 tbsp. unsweetened coconut powder
- ½ tsp. baking powder
- ¼ tsp. baking soda
- ½ tsp. sea salt

Preparation:

1. Preheat oven to 350F.

2. Grease 9 mini muffin cups with some almond oil and dust with cocoa.

3. In a bowl mix coconut sugar, water, vanilla pod and almond oil.

4. Place almonds, hemp seeds, cocoa, baking powder, baking soda and salt into a food processor and process until you have a smooth powder.

5. Add the previously mixed wet ingredients and pulse for few seconds until combined.

6. Spoon the mixture into the mini muffin cups.

7. Bake in the oven for 15-18 minutes.

8. Remove muffins from oven and let them rest for 10 minutes.

9. Transfer muffins to a wire rack to cool.

105. Almond Butter Squares

You will be extremely pleased with these almond butter squares.

The creamy almond butter mixed with coconut oil and chocolate makes it a delectable dessert.

Preparation time: 25 minutes

Setting time: 2 hours

Serves: 12 bars

Ingredients:

- 2 tbsp. coconut oil
- 1 cup and 2 tbsp. almond butter
- ¾ cup almond flour
- ¾ cup shredded coconut
- ¾ cup coconut palm sugar
- 4 ½ oz. dark chocolate 75% cocoa and over

Preparation:

1. Combine almond flour, shredded coconut and coconut sugar into a large bowl.

2. Melt 1 cup of almond butter and coconut oil over medium-low heat. If you want, you can melt it in the microwave for 15-30 seconds.

3. Once almond butter and coconut oil are melted, add to dry ingredients and mix well.

4. Take an 8"x 8" baking dish and press the mixture firmly into it.

5. Place 2 tablespoons of almond butter and the chocolate into a small saucepan and melt over medium-low heat. Alternatively, you can place into a bowl and melt in the microwave for 30 seconds.

6. Pour the melted chocolate over the pressed mixture and smooth out the top with a knife.

7. Refrigerate for at least 2 hours until the mixture has set.

8. Cut into 12 squares and serve or keep refrigerated for later.

106. Coconut Bites

These low-carb bites will be the perfect answer to your sweet cravings.

They can be consumed at room temperature, or you can serve them frozen for that ice cream-like texture. Yum!

Preparation time: 20 minutes

Serves: 16 bites

Ingredients:

For the Filling:

- ½ cup coconut oil - softened
- 4 cups grated unsweetened coconut
- 3 tbsp. coconut nectar

For the Coating:

- 1 ½ cup dark chocolate chips
- 1 tbsp. coconut oil

Preparation:

1. Put the filling ingredients into a food processor and process for several minutes until you have a smooth mixture.

2. Line an 8"x 8" container with baking paper.

3. Spread the filling around the container.

4. Put the filling in the freezer for 15 minutes to solidify.

5. In the meantime melt the chocolate together with the coconut oil. You can do this on the stove over low heat or in the microwave for 30 seconds.

6. Take the filling out of the freezer.

7. Get the filling out of the container by lifting the baking paper.

8. Cut the filling into 12 bitesize pieces of any shape you like.

9. Line a tray with baking paper.

10. Dip the bites one by one into the melted chocolate and rest them on the tray.

11. But in the freezer to set for 5 minutes.

12. Serve or store into an airtight container in the fridge or freezer for later.

Printed in Great Britain
by Amazon